College Girls Need Good Credit Too

Monthly Planner for Establishing and Maintaining Good Credit

DR. DONNA PRUDHOMME

CREDIT
EDUCATION SCHOOL

Written by Dr. Donna Prudhomme
Illustrated by Charlotte Pabalan

Printed in the United States of America
ISBN 978-1733-1188-3-5

www.crediteducationschool.com
info@crediteducationschool.com

Disclaimer

The author is not a lawyer. For legal advice, please seek an attorney as the contents of this book should not be construed as legal advice in any way. Every effort has been made to ensure the accuracy of the information within this book. However, we cannot be held liable for any omissions, errors, or inconsistencies. You are solely responsible for actions taken (or not taken) based on the information contained in this book.

This planner belongs to

Contents

Dedication

This planner is dedicated to my beloved sister, Nasheka Powell, affectionately known as Shay. Your presence is deeply missed every day, but I feel your spirit guiding me on this journey.

I ♡ Love you Sissy

Acknowledgements

First and foremost, I want to thank God for the opportunity to educate and empower girls around the world about the importance of credit.

I am deeply grateful to my loving husband, whose unwavering support has been a cornerstone of all my endeavors. You witnessed my exhaustion and the challenges of failed business ventures, yet you never told me to give up. I remember you saying, "You are always working hard, and eventually, something will happen." Your belief in me has been a constant source of strength and encouragement.

To my son and daughter, every pursuit I've undertaken has been for you, with the hope of making your lives better. Thank you for your patience and encouragement, especially during the times when things didn't go as planned. You have witnessed my struggles, and I am confident that you have learned from my mistakes. Your strength and resilience continue to inspire me, and I know these experiences will make you both even stronger.

Hey Girl, Hey!

I'm excited to introduce you to *College Girls Need Good Credit Too Planner* designed specifically for college students like you who are ready to take control of their financial future. While college is a time of academic growth, self-discovery, and new experiences, it's also the perfect time to start building a strong credit foundation.

When I was in college, companies were all over campus, pushing credit cards on us without warning us about the potential downsides. As a naive college student, I didn't fully grasp the long-term impact on my credit score and financial health. It wasn't until later that I understood the true cost of those seemingly innocent decisions. This experience has motivated me to educate others so they can make informed choices and avoid the same pitfalls.

Credit isn't just about getting approved for a credit card or a loan—it's about the opportunities and freedom it can provide. Good credit can help you rent your first apartment, secure a lower interest rate on a car loan, or even land a job after graduation. On the flip side, poor credit can create barriers that can take years to overcome.

That's why it's so important to start building good credit while you're in college. The habits you develop now will set the stage for your financial future. By understanding how credit works, using credit responsibly, and making informed financial decisions, you can create a credit history that will benefit you long after you've graduated.

I encourage you to dive into this planner with an open mind and a willingness to learn. The journey to good credit is one that requires patience, discipline, and commitment—but it's a journey well worth taking. You have the power to shape your financial destiny, and it all starts right here.

Wishing you success in all your endeavors, both financial and personal!

Dr. Donna Prudhomme

Dr. Donna Prudhomme
Board Certified Credit Consultant

"Your future self will thank you for the good credit habits you start today!"

Introduction

Welcome to the *College Girls Need Good Credit Too Planner*—a vital tool crafted to guide and support you as you navigate the exciting transition from college life to a financially independent future. This planner is designed specifically for college students like you, to help you build a solid foundation of credit management and financial responsibility.

As you embark on your academic journey, balancing coursework, social life, and possibly part-time work, managing your finances can seem overwhelming. But understanding and building good credit is crucial for achieving long-term financial stability and success. This planner will simplify that process, providing you with the essential tools and knowledge to make informed decisions about your credit.

Why Credit Matters: Establishing good credit early in your college years can set the stage for future financial opportunities. Whether it's applying for a credit card, renting an apartment, or securing a loan, having a strong credit history can make a significant difference. Good credit can lead to lower interest rates, better financial offers, and more opportunities as you move into adulthood.

What You'll Discover: This planner covers everything you need to know about credit–from understanding what credit is and how it affects your financial health, to practical tips for managing credit cards and avoiding common pitfalls. You'll also find advice on how to handle student loans, set financial goals, and build a budget that works for you.

Your Path to Financial Empowerment: Building good credit is a journey, not a destination. This planner is your companion along the way, helping you develop smart financial habits and stay on track. Remember, the choices you make today will have a lasting impact on your financial future.

Embrace this opportunity to take control of your financial health and make informed choices that will benefit you for years to come. Here's to a successful college experience and a promising financial future. Let's start this empowering journey together and build a path to financial success and independence!

PART ONE

Understanding How Your Mindset Can Affect Your Credit

1. Embrace Financial Responsibility

Entering college is a pivotal moment where you gain more independence and, with it, the responsibility of managing your own finances. Viewing this as an opportunity to learn and grow rather than a burden will set a positive tone for your financial journey. Understand that managing credit is a crucial part of this responsibility, so approach it with an open mind and eagerness to learn.

2. See Credit as a Tool, Not a Trap

Credit is a powerful tool that can help you achieve financial goals, but it requires careful management. Rather than fearing credit cards and loans, view them as instruments that, when used wisely, can help you build a strong financial foundation. Educate yourself about how credit works and how to use it responsibly to avoid common pitfalls.

3. Focus on Long-Term Goals

Building good credit isn't just about short-term benefits; it's about setting yourself up for future success. Keep in mind that the habits you develop now will impact your financial health for years to come. Set long-term financial goals and recognize that responsible credit management is a step towards achieving those goals.

4. Cultivate Financial Discipline

Developing discipline in managing your finances is key to maintaining good credit. This includes making timely payments, keeping credit card balances low, and avoiding unnecessary debt. Remember that financial discipline is a skill that improves with practice, so start small and build good habits over time.

5. Learn from Mistakes and Move Forward

Mistakes are a natural part of learning, and they can be valuable lessons in financial management. If you encounter setbacks, such as missed payments or high balances, view them as opportunities to learn and improve. Address any issues promptly and use them as stepping stones to build a stronger credit profile.

6. Take Ownership of Your Financial Future

Your credit journey is uniquely yours, and taking ownership of it means being proactive about managing and improving your credit. Stay informed about your credit report and score, set personal financial goals, and seek out resources and support when needed. By taking an active role, you empower yourself to shape your financial future.

7. Balance Financial Independence with Smart Choices

Being financially independent means making decisions that align with your values and goals. While it's exciting to have financial freedom, it's important to balance this with smart choices. Avoid impulsive spending and prioritize your financial well-being by making informed decisions that support your long-term goals.

8. Seek Guidance and Resources

Don't hesitate to seek out guidance and resources to help you navigate credit and financial management. Whether it's talking to a financial advisor, using educational tools, or connecting with peers, leveraging available resources can provide valuable insights and support.

9. Stay Positive and Persistent

Building good credit and managing finances effectively can be challenging, but maintaining a positive and persistent mindset will help you stay motivated. Celebrate your progress, no matter how small, and keep pushing forward towards your financial goals.

10. Remember the Bigger Picture

Good credit is just one aspect of your overall financial health. Keep in mind that it's part of a larger picture that includes budgeting, saving, investing, and planning for the future. Integrate credit management into your broader financial strategy to achieve a balanced and successful financial life.

By adopting a proactive and positive mindset towards credit, you'll be better equipped to make informed decisions and build a solid financial foundation. Embrace the journey with confidence and enthusiasm, knowing that your efforts today will pave the way for a successful and financially secure future.

"College prepares you for the world; good credit opens the doors to it!"

PART TWO

Understanding Credit

What is Credit?

Credit is the ability to borrow money or access goods and services with the understanding that you will pay back the lender or provider over time, often with interest. It's a financial tool that allows you to make purchases or access services now and pay for them later. Credit can come in various forms, such as credit cards, loans, or lines of credit.

Components of a Credit Profile

Credit is typically assessed through several components, including:

- **Payment History:** Whether you've made payments on time.
- **Credit Utilization:** The ratio of your current credit balances to your credit limits.
- **Length of Credit History:** How long you've been using credit.
- **Credit Mix:** The variety of credit accounts you have, such as credit cards, auto loans, or mortgages.
- **New Credit:** Recent credit inquiries or new accounts that can impact your score.

Types of Credit

Credit comes in several types, each serving different financial needs:

- **Revolving Credit:** Such as credit cards, where you can borrow up to a certain limit and repay monthly.
- **Installment Credit:** Like student loans or mortgages, where you borrow a fixed amount and make regular payments over time.
- **Service Credit:** Credit extended by service providers, like utility companies, allowing you to use services before paying for them.

How to Get Credit?

To establish credit, you can start by applying for a secured credit card, becoming an authorized user on someone else's account, or taking out a small loan. Once you have credit, it's important to use it responsibly by making timely payments and keeping your balances low.

Why is Credit Important?

Credit is crucial because it affects your ability to borrow money, rent an apartment, get a job, and even qualify for certain services. Good credit can lead to lower interest rates and better financial opportunities, while poor credit can limit your options.

What is Good Credit?

Good credit typically refers to a credit score that falls within the range of 670 to 739 on a FICO scale of 300 to 850. It indicates that you have a history of managing credit responsibly and are likely to repay borrowed money.

Impact of a Good Credit Score

A good credit score can result in:

- Lower interest rates on loans and credit cards.
- Higher credit limits.
- Easier approval for rental applications.
- Better insurance rates.
- Increased negotiating power.

What is Bad Credit?

Bad credit generally refers to a credit score below 580 on the FICO scale. It indicates a history of late payments, high credit balances, or other financial mismanagement, making it harder to borrow money or get approved for credit.

Impact of a Bad Credit Score

A bad credit score can lead to:

- Higher interest rates.
- Difficulty securing loans or credit cards.
- Lower credit limits.
- Challenges in renting an apartment.
- Potential job application issues.

Tips to Improve Bad Credit

Improving bad credit involves:

- Paying your bills on time.
- Reducing outstanding balances.
- Avoiding new credit applications while you work on improving your credit.
- Disputing inaccuracies on your credit report.
- Seeking credit counseling if needed.

Managing Credit Responsibly

Responsible credit management means consistently paying your bills on time, keeping your credit utilization low (below 30% of your available credit), and regularly reviewing your credit reports to catch and correct errors.

Credit Gem

Keep your credit utilization between 1-10% to maximize your credit profile and boost your score.

What is FICO?

FICO stands for **Fair Isaac Corporation,** the company that developed one of the most widely used credit scoring models. A FICO score is a three-digit number 300-850 that lenders use to assess your credit risk.

What is a Credit Score?

A credit score is a numerical representation of your creditworthiness, based on your credit history. It helps lenders determine how likely you are to repay a loan or credit card balance.

Why is a Credit Score Important?

Your credit score is important because it influences your ability to borrow money, the interest rates you'll pay, and your eligibility for certain jobs, rentals, and services.

Credit Gem

Your credit score is your financial reputation—protect and manage it wisely.

How is a Credit Score Calculated?

A credit score is calculated based on several factors, including:

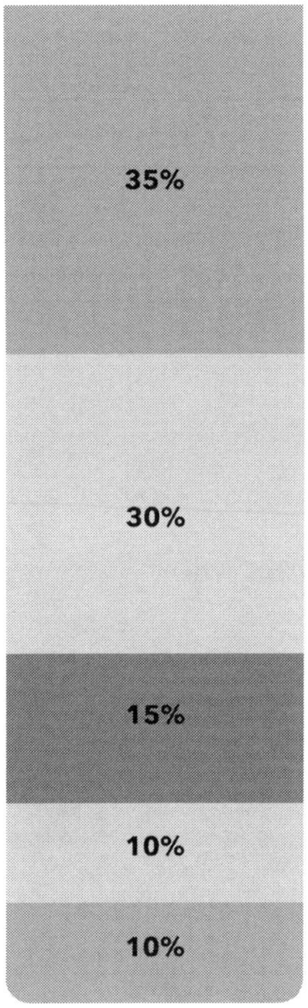

Payment History (35%) | 192.5 Points
Your record of paying bills on time.

Credit Utilization (30%) | 165 Points
The amount of available credit you're using.

Length of Credit History (15%) | 82.5 Points
How long you've been using credit.

Credit Mix (10%) | 55 Points
The variety of credit accounts you have.

New Credit (10%) | | 55 Points
Recent credit inquiries and new accounts.

What are the Credit Score Ranges?

Credit scores generally fall within these ranges:

Poor (300-579)

- A poor credit score indicates significant credit risk and may result from late payments, defaults, or other negative credit events.
- Individuals with poor credit scores may have difficulty obtaining credit and, if approved, may face high interest rates and unfavorable terms.

Fair (580-669)

- A fair credit score shows moderate credit risk.
- Lenders may offer credit but with higher interest rates and less favorable terms.

Good (670-739)

- A good credit score indicates lower credit risk.
- Borrowers are likely to be approved for credit with reasonable interest rates and terms.

Very Good (740-799)

- A very good credit score reflects a strong credit history and low credit risk.
- Individuals are likely to receive favorable loan terms and interest rates.

Excellent (800-850)

- An excellent credit score demonstrates minimal credit risk.
- Borrowers with excellent scores typically receive the best interest rates and credit terms.

Tips to Build and Maintain Good Credit

To build and maintain good credit:

- Always pay your bills on time.
- Keep your credit utilization low.
- Avoid opening too many new accounts in a short period.
- Regularly monitor your credit report for accuracy.
- Maintain a mix of different types of credit.

What is Credit Monitoring?

Credit monitoring is a service that tracks your credit reports for any changes, such as new accounts, inquiries, or late payments. It helps you stay on top of your credit and spot potential issues, such as identity theft, early.

Why is Credit Monitoring Important?

Credit monitoring is important because it allows you to detect and respond to changes in your credit report quickly, helping to prevent identity theft and maintain a good credit score.

How to Choose a Credit Monitoring Service

When choosing a credit monitoring service, consider:

- **Coverage:** Ensure the service monitors all three major credit bureaus.
- **Alerts:** Look for timely alerts for significant changes.
- **Cost:** Compare prices and features.
- **Reputation:** Research the service's reputation and customer reviews.

Who are the Credit Bureaus?

The three major credit bureaus in the United States are:

Equifax   Experian   TransUnion

These bureaus collect and maintain information about your credit history, which they use to generate your credit reports and scores.

How to Contact the Credit Bureaus?

You can contact the credit bureaus through their websites, by phone, or by mail:

- Equifax: www.equifax.com, 1-800-685-1111
- Experian: www.experian.com, 1-888-397-3742
- TransUnion: www.transunion.com, 1-800-916-8800

Each bureau allows you to request a copy of your credit report, dispute errors, and place fraud alerts or credit freezes on your account.

"College is the time to invest in knowledge and your credit score—both pay off big!"

PART THREE

Understanding the Credit Report

What is a Credit Report?

A credit report is a detailed summary of your credit history, compiled by credit reporting agencies. It includes information on your credit accounts, payment history, credit inquiries, and any public records such as bankruptcies. Lenders, employers, and others use this report to evaluate your creditworthiness and financial responsibility.

How to Pull Your Credit Report?

You can pull your credit report from the three major credit bureaus–Equifax, Experian, and TransUnion–once a year for free at AnnualCreditReport.com. Additionally, some financial institutions and credit monitoring services offer access to your credit report as part of their service.

AnnualCreditReport.com

AnnualCreditReport.com is the only website authorized by federal law to provide free credit reports from the three major credit reporting agencies–Equifax, Experian, and TransUnion. Here's a guide on how to use AnnualCreditReport.com effectively

1. What is AnnualCreditReport.com?

AnnualCreditReport.com is a central site created by the federal government to allow consumers to access their credit reports from the three major credit bureaus once a year at no cost. It is the only website specifically mandated by the **Fair Credit Reporting Act (FCRA)** to provide free credit reports.

2. How to Request Your Free Credit Report?

- **Visit the Website:** Go to AnnualCreditReport.com
- **Provide Personal Information:** Enter your name, address, Social Security number, and date of birth to verify your identity.
- **Select Your Credit Reports:** Choose to receive your credit report from Equifax, Experian, and TransUnion. You can request reports from all three at once or stagger them throughout the year.
- **Answer Security Questions:** You may need to answer questions related to your credit history to confirm your identity.
- **Review Your Reports:** Once you access your reports, review them carefully for accuracy and completeness.

3. Why Check Your Credit Reports?

- **Detect Errors:** Ensure that all the information on your credit report is accurate and up-to-date. Incorrect information can affect your credit score and financial health.
- **Monitor for Identity Theft:** Look for unfamiliar accounts or inquiries that may indicate fraudulent activity.
- **Understand Your Credit Profile:** Knowing what's on your credit report helps you manage your credit more effectively and address any issues before they impact your credit score.

4. How Often Should You Check Your Credit Reports?

- **Annually:** It's recommended to check your credit reports at least once a year. By spreading out your requests, you can monitor your credit throughout the year.

- **Before Major Financial Decisions:** Check your credit report before applying for a loan, credit card, or rental agreement to ensure there are no surprises.

5. What to Do If You Find Errors

- **Dispute the Error:** If you find inaccuracies, you can dispute them with the credit bureau that issued the report. Each bureau has a process for handling disputes, which can usually be done online, by phone, or by mail.
- **Provide Documentation:** Include supporting documents to substantiate your claim when filing a dispute.
- **Follow Up:** Monitor the dispute process to ensure that the error is corrected.

6. Protecting Your Credit Information

- **Secure Your Personal Information:** Ensure that you are on a secure network and using a trusted device when accessing your credit reports.
- **Be Cautious of Scams:** Be wary of websites or services claiming to offer free credit reports but asking for payment or personal information. Always use AnnualCreditReport.com for your free annual reports.

7. Additional Services

- **Credit Scores:** AnnualCreditReport.com provides free credit reports, but not credit scores. You can request your credit score from each bureau separately or obtain it through other services or credit card issuers.

Credit Gem

AnnualCreditReport.com is a valuable resource for managing your credit health. Regularly reviewing your credit reports ensures that you stay informed and can address any issues that may arise.

How to Review Your Credit Report?

When reviewing your credit report, check for:

- **Accuracy of Personal Information:** Ensure your name, address, and Social Security number are correct.
- **Account Information:** Verify that all listed accounts are yours and that the balances, payment history, and credit limits are accurate.
- **Credit Inquiries:** Look for inquiries that you did not authorize.
- **Public Records:** Confirm that any public records, such as bankruptcies or judgments, are reported accurately.
- **Errors:** If you find any inaccuracies, dispute them with the credit bureau that issued the report.

Who's Responsible for Reporting Information to the Credit Reporting Agencies?

Creditors, such as banks, credit card companies, and loan providers, are responsible for reporting your credit activity to the credit reporting agencies. They send regular updates on your account status, payment history, and credit limits to the bureaus.

Who Can Access Your Credit Information?

Your credit information can be accessed by:

- **Lenders:** When you apply for a loan or credit card.
- **Landlords:** When you apply to rent an apartment.
- **Insurance Companies:** When you apply for insurance.
- **Employers:** With your permission, during the hiring process.
- **Government Agencies:** For certain legal or regulatory purposes.

Who Can't Access Your Credit Information?

Your credit information cannot be accessed by anyone without a **legitimate business need or your explicit permission.** This means that friends, family members, or unauthorized individuals cannot legally view your credit report.

How to Protect Your Credit Information?

To protect your credit information:

- **Monitor Your Credit Regularly:** Check your credit report for unauthorized activity.
- **Use Credit Freezes:** Place a freeze on your credit to prevent new accounts from being opened in your name.
- **Enable Fraud Alerts:** Notify the credit bureaus if you suspect your identity has been stolen.
- **Be Cautious with Personal Information:** Avoid sharing your Social Security number or other sensitive data unless absolutely necessary.

What are Credit Inquiries?

Credit inquiries occur when someone checks your credit report, usually when you apply for a loan, credit card, or other services. There are two types of inquiries: **hard inquiries** and **soft inquiries.**

Hard vs. Soft Inquiries

- **Hard Inquiries:** These occur when a lender checks your credit report to make a lending decision. Hard inquiries can slightly lower your credit score and stay on your report for up to two years.
- **Soft Inquiries:** These occur when you check your own credit report, or when a company checks it for promotional purposes. Soft inquiries do not affect your credit score.

What 5 Factors Make Up the Credit Score?

A credit score is typically calculated based on the following five factors:

- **Payment History (35%) | 192.5 Points:** Your record of on-time payments.
- **Credit Utilization (30%) | 165 Points:** The ratio of your current debt to your credit limits.
- **Length of Credit History (15%) | 82.5 Points:** How long your credit accounts have been open.
- **Credit Mix (10%) | 55 Points** The variety of credit accounts you have.
- **New Credit (10%) | 55 Points** Recent inquiries and newly opened accounts.

What is Permissible Purpose?

Permissible purpose refers to the legal reasons someone can access your credit report, as defined by the **Fair Credit Reporting Act (FCRA).** Examples include when a lender evaluates you for a loan, when an employer conducts a background check with your consent, or when a landlord screens your rental application.

Employers

Employers may request to review your credit report as part of a background check, particularly for roles involving financial responsibility. However, they must obtain your written consent before accessing your credit information.

Illegal Requests for Your Credit Report

It is illegal for anyone to access your credit report without a permissible purpose or your explicit permission. If you suspect unauthorized access, you should report it to the credit bureaus and take steps to secure your credit information.

Reading Your Credit Report

Reading your credit report involves understanding its sections:

- **Personal Information:** Your name, address, Social Security number, and employment history. You should only have 1 name and address.
- **Credit Accounts:** Details of your credit cards, loans, and other credit accounts, including payment history and current balances.
- **Credit Inquiries:** A list of who has accessed your credit report and when.
- **Public Records:** Any bankruptcies, liens, or judgments that may impact your creditworthiness.
- **Account Status:** Whether your accounts are open, closed, or in collections.

By regularly reviewing and understanding your credit report, you can maintain control over your financial health and take steps to improve your credit as needed.

"Mastering credit in college is like earning extra credit for your future!"

PART FOUR

Understanding Consumer Law

Incomplete or Inaccurate Information

Incomplete or inaccurate information on your credit report can negatively impact your credit score and financial reputation. This can include incorrect personal details, errors in account balances, or outdated information. It's crucial to regularly review your credit report and address any discrepancies to ensure that your credit profile accurately reflects your financial history.

FCRA (Fair Credit Reporting Act)

The **Fair Credit Reporting Act (FCRA)** is a federal law that governs how credit information is collected, used, and shared. It ensures that the information on your credit report is accurate, fair, and private. Key provisions of the FCRA include:

- **Right to Access:** You have the right to obtain a free copy of your credit report annually from each of the major credit bureaus.
- **Accuracy and Privacy:** Credit reporting agencies must ensure the accuracy and privacy of the information in your credit report.

- **Dispute Process:** If you find inaccuracies on your credit report, you have the right to dispute them. The credit bureau must investigate and correct any errors within a reasonable time.

Responsibilities of the Furnishers

Furnishers are entities that provide information to credit reporting agencies, such as lenders and creditors. Their responsibilities under the FCRA include:

- **Accuracy:** Furnishers must ensure that the information they provide is accurate and up-to-date.
- **Timely Updates:** They must update or correct information promptly if they become aware of inaccuracies.
- **Investigation:** When notified of a dispute, furnishers must investigate the claim and report the findings to the credit reporting agency.

Responsibilities of the Consumer Reporting Agencies

Consumer reporting agencies, or credit bureaus, have specific responsibilities under the FCRA:

- **Accuracy:** They must ensure that the information they maintain is accurate and complete.
- **Investigation:** Upon receiving a dispute, they must investigate the issue and resolve it within a reasonable timeframe, usually 30 days.
- **Privacy:** They must protect the confidentiality of your credit report and only release it to parties with a legitimate need or with your explicit permission.

FDCPA (Fair Debt Collection Practices Act)

The **Fair Debt Collection Practices Act (FDCPA)** is a federal law that regulates the actions of third-party debt collectors. It is designed to protect consumers from abusive, deceptive, and unfair debt collection practices. Key provisions include:

- **Prohibition of Harassment:** Debt collectors cannot harass, oppress, or abuse you. This includes threats, obscene language, or repeated calls.

- **Debt Verification:** You have the right to request verification of the debt. The collector must provide proof that you owe the debt and that they have the authority to collect it.
- **Fair Practices:** Collectors must treat you fairly and respectfully, and they must follow specific guidelines about when and how they can contact you.

How Does Consumer Law Protect Me?

Consumer law provides several protections to ensure fair treatment and accuracy in your credit dealings:

- **Accuracy and Transparency:** Laws like the FCRA require credit reporting agencies to maintain accurate credit information and provide you with access to your credit reports.
- **Dispute Rights:** You have the right to dispute inaccuracies and must be notified of the outcome of these disputes.
- **Debt Collection Protections:** The FDCPA protects you from abusive or deceptive practices by debt collectors, ensuring that any collection activity is conducted fairly and respectfully.
- **Privacy:** Your credit information must be kept private and only accessed by authorized entities.

By understanding these laws and your rights, you can better manage and protect your credit profile and handle any issues that arise with your credit report or debt collection practices.

"Just like your GPA, your credit score reflects your hard work —aim high!"

PART FIVE

Understanding the Dispute Process

1. Obtain Your Credit Report: Start by getting a copy of all three of your credit reports from AnnualCreditReport.com. Review them carefully to identify any errors or inaccuracies.

2. Gather Documentation: Collect any supporting documents that prove the information on your credit report is incorrect. This can include account statements, receipts, or correspondence with creditors.

3. Prepare Your Dispute Letter: Write a clear and concise dispute letter. Include details such as your name, address, and Social Security number, the specific items you are disputing, and a brief explanation of why you believe the information is incorrect. Attach copies of your supporting documents.

4. Send Your Dispute: Mail your dispute letter along with any supporting documentation to the credit bureau that is reporting the incorrect information. Be sure to send it via certified mail with a return receipt requested, so you have proof of when the bureau received your dispute.

5. Monitor the Dispute: The credit bureau typically has 30 days to investigate and respond to your dispute. During this time, they will review your evidence, contact the furnisher of the information, and make a determination. Keep track of the progress and any correspondence.

6. Review the Outcome: Once the investigation is complete, the credit bureau will send you the results in writing. If the disputed information is corrected or removed, you'll receive an updated credit report. If the dispute is not resolved in your favor, you have the right to add a statement to your credit report explaining your side of the story.

Dispute Checklist

- ☐ **Obtain Your Credit Report:** Ensure you have a current copy from all three credit bureaus.
- ☐ **Identify Errors:** Note all inaccuracies or outdated information.
- ☐ **Gather Documentation:** Collect relevant documents to support your dispute.
- ☐ **Write a Dispute Letter:** Include your personal details, a description of the error, and copies of supporting documents.
- ☐ **Send Dispute:** Mail your dispute letter to the appropriate credit bureau with proof of delivery.
- ☐ **Track Dispute:** Monitor the status of your dispute and keep records of all communications.
- ☐ **Review Results:** Check the outcome of your dispute and update your records if necessary.

Where to Send Your Dispute Letters

Equifax

- Mailing Address: Equifax Information Services LLC, P.O. Box 740256, Atlanta, GA 30374
- Website: www.equifax.com/personal/credit-report-services

Experian

- Mailing Address: Experian, P.O. Box 4500, Allen, TX 75013
- Website: www.experian.com/disputes

TransUnion

- Mailing Address: TransUnion LLC, P.O. Box 2000, Chester, PA 19016
- Website: www.transunion.com/credit-dispute

By following these steps and utilizing the provided checklist, you can effectively manage the dispute process and ensure your credit report accurately reflects your financial history.

"Balancing books and budgets—college life is the perfect time to build strong credit!"

PART SIX

Understanding How to Build Credit in College

Why Do Credit Card Companies Target College Students?

Credit card companies target college students for several reasons:

1. Long-Term Customer Potential: College students represent a long-term opportunity for credit card companies. By acquiring young customers early, companies hope to build a lasting relationship and create brand loyalty that lasts well into their professional careers.

2. Growing Market: As students transition into adulthood, they begin managing their own finances and making financial decisions independently. Credit card companies aim to capture this emerging market while students are still developing their financial habits.

3. Building Credit History Early: By introducing students to credit early, credit card companies encourage them to start building their credit history. A positive credit history can lead to more substantial credit products and financial benefits in the future.

4. Higher Interest Rates and Fees: College students, who often have limited credit histories, may be offered higher interest rates and fees compared to more experienced credit users. This can be profitable for credit card companies, especially if students carry balances or accrue fees.

5. Educational Programs: Credit card companies often offer financial education resources, which they use to attract college students. These programs can be a way to market their products while helping students learn about credit management.

6. Limited Financial Experience: Many college students are new to managing credit and may not fully understand the implications of credit card usage. Credit card companies see this as an opportunity to introduce their products before students gain more financial knowledge.

By understanding why credit card companies target college students, you can be more prepared to navigate credit offers and make informed decisions about managing credit while in college.

How to Build Credit in College

Building credit while in college can set you up for financial success in the future. Here are some strategies to help you establish and maintain good credit:

Get a Credit Card

- Start with a Student Credit Card: Look for credit cards designed for college students, which may have lower credit limits and easier approval requirements.
- Consider a Secured Credit Card: If you're unable to get an unsecured card, a secured credit card, which requires a deposit as collateral, can be a good option to build credit.

Use Credit Responsibly

- Make Payments on Time: Always pay your credit card bill by the due date to avoid late fees and negative marks on your credit report.

- Keep Balances Low: Aim to use no more than 30% of your credit limit to maintain a good credit utilization ratio. Remember, 1-10% credit utilization is ideal to maximize your credit profile and boost your credit score.

Build a Positive Payment History

- Set Up Automatic Payments: To ensure you never miss a payment, set up automatic payments for at least the minimum amount due.
- Pay More Than the Minimum: If possible, pay more than the minimum balance to reduce your debt faster and avoid accumulating interest.

Monitor Your Credit Report

- Check Your Credit Regularly: Obtain free credit reports from the major bureaus (Equifax, Experian, TransUnion) at AnnualCreditReport.com and review them for accuracy.
- Address Errors Promptly: Dispute any inaccuracies on your credit report as soon as you spot them.

Build a Positive Credit Mix

- Consider a Small Loan: If feasible, take out a small loan (like a student loan) and make timely payments. This can diversify your credit profile.
- Avoid Over-Applying: Too many credit inquiries can negatively affect your credit score. Apply for credit only when necessary.

Be Strategic with Credit Applications

- Apply for Credit Wisely: Only apply for credit cards or loans you need and can manage responsibly. Each application results in a hard inquiry on your credit report.
- Understand Terms and Conditions: Read and understand the terms of any credit product before applying

Use Student Discounts Wisely

- Leverage Discounts: Use credit cards to take advantage of student discounts and rewards, but ensure you pay off the balances to avoid debt.

Avoid Common Pitfalls

- Don't Accumulate Debt: Avoid spending beyond your means or using credit for non-essential purchases.
- Stay Informed: Educate yourself about interest rates, fees, and the impact of credit utilization on your score.

Consider Becoming an Authorized User

- On a Family Member's Account: If a responsible family member adds you as an authorized user on their account, their positive payment history can benefit your credit score.

Plan for the Future

- Understand Student Loan Impact: Know how student loans will affect your credit and make sure to manage them responsibly.
- Build a Budget: Create a budget to manage your spending and savings while you're in college.

By following these steps, you can build a strong credit foundation while still in college, which will benefit you in future financial endeavors such as applying for a car loan, a mortgage, or other types of credit.

What Are the Cons of College Students Having Credit Cards?

While credit cards can offer numerous benefits, such as building credit and providing financial flexibility, they also come with potential drawbacks for college students. Here are some of the cons to be aware of:

High Interest Rates

- **Costly Debt:** Credit cards often come with high interest rates, especially for students who may not have established credit histories. This can lead to expensive debt if balances are not paid off in full each month.

Risk of Accumulating Debt

- **Ease of Spending:** The convenience of credit cards can lead to overspending and accumulating debt. Without a strong budget or spending plan, students may find themselves struggling with high balances.

Impact on Credit Score

- **Negative Effects of Mismanagement:** Late payments, high credit utilization, and accumulating debt can negatively impact a student's credit score. A poor credit history can affect future financial opportunities, such as loans or rental applications.

Potential for Financial Stress

- **Overwhelming Financial Burden:** Managing credit card debt can be stressful, particularly if a student is juggling multiple financial responsibilities like tuition, rent, and living expenses.

High Fees

- **Additional Costs:** Credit cards can come with various fees, including annual fees, late payment fees, and foreign transaction fees. These fees can add up and create additional financial strain.

Debt Collection Risks

- **Potential for Collection:** Failure to manage credit card debt responsibly can lead to collection actions, which can be stressful and harm a student's credit score further.

Impact on Financial Independence

- **Dependency on Credit:** Relying too heavily on credit cards can lead to a dependency on borrowed funds, potentially hindering the development of healthy financial habits and independence.

Potential for Identity Theft

- **Increased Risk:** Students, like all consumers, are at risk of identity theft. Credit cards can be a target for thieves, leading to potential financial and personal information issues.

Limited Understanding of Credit Management

- **Lack of Experience:** College students may lack experience in managing credit and understanding the full implications of credit card usage, which can lead to poor financial decisions.

Temptation to Live Beyond Means

- **Increased Spending Temptation:** Credit cards can tempt students to make purchases they cannot afford, leading to unnecessary debt and financial difficulties.

Long-Term Financial Impact

- **Debt Accumulation Over Time:** If not managed carefully, credit card debt accumulated during college can follow students into their post-graduation life, affecting their financial stability and future goals.

By being aware of these potential drawbacks, college students can take proactive steps to manage their credit cards responsibly and avoid the pitfalls associated with credit card usage

Understanding the Biggest Credit Mistakes College Students Make – and How to Avoid Them

As college students begin to manage their own finances, they often encounter pitfalls that can negatively impact their credit. Here are some of the biggest credit mistakes college students make and tips on how to avoid them:

Overspending and Accumulating Debt

- **Mistake:** Using credit cards for non-essential purchases or overspending on everyday expenses can lead to high credit card balances and accumulating debt.
- **How to Avoid:** Create a budget to track your income and expenses. Use your credit card only for planned purchases and within your budget. Aim to pay off the balance in full each month to avoid interest charges.

Missing Payments

- **Mistake:** Failing to make credit card payments on time can result in late fees and damage to your credit score.
- **How to Avoid:** Set up automatic payments for at least the minimum amount due. Alternatively, set reminders or use a financial app to keep track of payment due dates.

Carrying a High Credit Utilization Ratio

- **Mistake:** Using a large percentage of your credit limit can negatively impact your credit score.
- **How to Avoid:** Aim to keep your credit utilization below 30% of your total credit limit. Pay down your balances regularly and consider requesting a credit limit increase if needed. Credit utilization between 1-10% is best.

Applying for Too Many Credit Cards

- **Mistake:** Applying for multiple credit cards in a short period can lead to numerous hard inquiries on your credit report, which can lower your credit score.
- **How to Avoid:** Only apply for credit cards you genuinely need and do so sparingly. Research your options and choose cards that fit your financial needs and goals.

Neglecting to Monitor Credit Reports

- **Mistake:** Failing to review your credit reports regularly can result in missing errors or fraudulent activity.
- **How to Avoid:** Obtain free copies of your credit reports from the three major credit bureaus (Equifax, Experian, TransUnion) annually at AnnualCreditReport.com. Review them for accuracy and dispute any inaccuracies promptly.

Not Understanding the Terms and Conditions

- **Mistake:** Not fully understanding the terms, fees, and interest rates associated with a credit card can lead to unexpected costs and financial difficulties.

- **How to Avoid:** Read the credit card agreement thoroughly before applying. Familiarize yourself with the interest rates, fees, and payment terms to avoid surprises.

Using Credit for Emergencies Only

- **Mistake:** Not relying on credit cards only for emergencies can lead to high balances and difficulty managing debt when emergencies arise.
- **How to Avoid:** Build an emergency fund to cover unexpected expenses. Use credit cards for planned purchases and emergencies as a last resort.

Ignoring the Impact of Credit on Financial Goals

- **Mistake:** Not considering how credit card use affects long-term financial goals, such as buying a car or securing a loan.
- **How to Avoid:** Understand how your credit card behavior affects your credit score and financial goals. Make responsible credit decisions with your future financial needs in mind.

Overlooking Credit Card Fees

- **Mistake:** Ignoring fees such as annual fees, late payment fees, and foreign transaction fees can lead to unnecessary costs.
- **How to Avoid:** Be aware of any fees associated with your credit card and find ways to avoid them. Choose cards with no annual fee or fees that align with your spending habits.

Failing to Build a Positive Credit History

- **Mistake:** Not using credit responsibly or not using credit at all can lead to a limited credit history and lower credit scores.
- **How to Avoid:** Use credit cards responsibly by making timely payments and keeping balances low. Consider other credit-building options, such as small loans or secured credit cards, to establish a positive credit history.

By understanding these common credit mistakes and taking proactive steps to avoid them, college students can build a strong credit foundation and manage their finances more effectively.

"Your college degree and good credit are the ultimate power duo—unlock your future with both!"

PART SEVEN

Understanding Student Loans During College

Student loans are a common way to finance higher education, but they come with responsibilities and potential long-term impacts. Here's what you need to know about managing student loans while in college:

1. Types of Student Loans

Federal Student Loans: These are loans provided by the U.S. Department of Education. They generally have lower interest rates and more flexible repayment options compared to private loans. Key types include:

- **Direct Subsidized Loans:** For students with financial need; the government pays the interest while you're in school.
- **Direct Unsubsidized Loans:** Available to all students regardless of financial need; interest accrues while you're in school.
- **Direct PLUS Loans:** For graduate students or parents of undergraduates; requires a credit check and has higher interest rates.

Private Student Loans: Offered by banks, credit unions, and other financial institutions. These loans can have varying interest rates, fees, and repayment terms. They usually require a credit check and may not offer the same flexible repayment options as federal loans.

2. Understanding Loan Terms

- **Interest Rates:** The cost of borrowing money, expressed as a percentage of the loan amount. Federal loans typically have fixed interest rates, while private loans may have fixed or variable rates.
- **Repayment Terms:** The length of time over which you will repay the loan. Federal loans usually offer various repayment plans, while private loans may have fewer options.
- **Fees:** Some loans may have origination fees or other costs. Understand all associated fees before accepting a loan.

3. Borrowing Responsibly

- **Only Borrow What You Need:** Determine your actual funding needs by creating a budget that includes tuition, fees, and living expenses. Avoid borrowing more than necessary.
- **Consider Your Future Earnings:** Think about your potential future income and how it will affect your ability to repay the loan. Borrowing too much can lead to financial strain after graduation.

4. Managing Your Loans While in School

- **Keep Track of Your Loans:** Use the National Student Loan Data System (NSLDS) to track your federal loans. For private loans, keep records from your lender.
- **Understand Your Interest:** For unsubsidized loans, interest accrues while you're in school. Consider paying off the interest periodically to avoid it capitalizing (being added to your principal balance).

5. Repayment Plans

Federal Loan Repayment Plans: Options include:

- **Standard Repayment Plan:** Fixed payments over 10 years.

- **Graduated Repayment Plan:** Payments start lower and increase every two years.
- **Income-Driven Repayment Plans:** Payments based on your income and family size, with potential for loan forgiveness after 20-25 years.

6. Deferment and Forbearance

- **Deferment:** Allows you to temporarily postpone payments on federal loans under certain conditions, such as returning to school or experiencing economic hardship.
- **Forbearance:** Temporarily reduces or pauses payments due to financial difficulties, but interest continues to accrue.

7. Loan Forgiveness and Repayment Assistance

- **Public Service Loan Forgiveness (PSLF):** Forgives remaining loan balance after 120 qualifying payments while working in a qualifying public service job.
- **Teacher Loan Forgiveness:** Offers forgiveness for teachers who work in low income schools for five consecutive years.
- **Income-Driven Repayment (IDR) Forgiveness:** Potentially forgives remaining loan balance after 20-25 years of qualifying payments under an IDR plan.

8. Preparing for Loan Repayment

- **Know Your Repayment Start Date:** Federal loans typically enter repayment six months after graduation, leaving school, or dropping below half-time status.
- **Create a Repayment Plan:** Begin planning for repayment before you graduate. Consider your monthly payments and how they fit into your post-graduation budget.

9. Avoiding Default

- **Communicate with Your Lender:** If you're struggling with payments, contact your loan servicer to discuss options and avoid default.
- **Explore Repayment Options:** Utilize deferment, forbearance, or income-driven repayment plans if needed to manage payments.

10. Staying Informed

- **Educate Yourself:** Understand the terms of your loans and keep up-to-date on any changes in federal loan policies or repayment options.
- **Seek Advice:** Use resources like financial aid offices, student loan counselors, or financial advisors for guidance on managing your student loans effectively.

By understanding these aspects of student loans and managing them wisely, you can minimize financial stress and set yourself up for a successful financial future after graduation.

“Studying hard? Don’t forget to give your credit score a little extra attention too!”

PART EIGHT

Understanding Life After College

Transitioning from college to the professional world brings new financial responsibilities and opportunities. Here's what to consider as you navigate life after college:

1. Managing Student Loan Repayment

- **Start Repayment on Time:** Federal student loans typically enter repayment six months after you graduate or drop below half-time status. Ensure you know your repayment start date and plan accordingly.
- **Choose the Right Repayment Plan:** Explore repayment options such as Standard, Graduated, or Income-Driven Repayment Plans to find the one that best fits your financial situation. Private loans may have different terms, so review those carefully.
- **Make Payments on Time:** Set up automatic payments to avoid missing due dates and accruing late fees. Timely payments help maintain a positive credit history.

2. Building and Maintaining Good Credit

- **Monitor Your Credit:** Regularly check your credit reports for accuracy and track your credit score. You can obtain free reports from Equifax, Experian, and TransUnion annually at AnnualCreditReport.com.

- **Manage Your Credit Utilization:** Keep your credit card balances low and avoid maxing out your credit limits. Aim to use no more than 30% of your available credit. However, 1-10% credit utilization is best to have a higher score.
- **Continue Responsible Credit Use:** Use credit cards wisely, make timely payments, and avoid carrying high balances to build and maintain a strong credit history.

3. Creating a Budget

- **Develop a Budget:** Create a detailed budget to manage your income and expenses. Include rent, utilities, transportation, groceries, and savings. Adjust your budget as needed based on your income and financial goals.
- **Track Your Spending:** Use budgeting apps or tools to monitor your spending and ensure you stay within your budget.

4. Building an Emergency Fund

- **Save for Unexpected Expenses:** Aim to build an emergency fund with at least three to six months' worth of living expenses. This fund can help cover unexpected costs, such as medical emergencies or job loss.
- **Automate Savings:** Set up automatic transfers to your savings account to build your emergency fund consistently.

5. Planning for Retirement

- **Start Early:** Begin contributing to retirement accounts, such as a 401(k) or IRA, as early as possible. Even small contributions can grow significantly over time due to compound interest.
- **Take Advantage of Employer Benefits:** If your employer offers a 401(k) match, contribute enough to receive the full match, as it's essentially free money for your retirement.

6. Managing Health Insurance

- **Understand Your Options:** Review your health insurance options, including employer sponsored plans, private insurance, and government programs. Ensure you have adequate coverage to meet your health needs.
- **Explore Marketplace Plans:** If you're not covered by an employer plan, explore options through the Health Insurance Marketplace or Medicaid, depending on your eligibility.

7. Building a Professional Network

- **Network Actively:** Build and maintain a professional network through industry events, social media, and alumni associations. Networking can open doors to job opportunities and career advancement.
- **Seek Mentorship:** Find mentors who can provide guidance, advice, and support as you navigate your career path.

8. Setting Financial Goals

- **Short-Term Goals:** Set achievable short-term goals, such as saving for a vacation or paying off credit card debt.
- **Long-Term Goals:** Establish long-term goals, such as purchasing a home or investing for retirement. Create a plan to work towards these goals and adjust as needed.

9. Understanding Taxes

- **File Your Taxes:** Learn about your tax responsibilities, including filing deadlines and available deductions or credits. Consider using tax preparation software or consulting a tax professional.
- **Plan for Tax Payments:** Set aside money for taxes if you're self-employed or have additional sources of income.

10. Managing Debt Wisely

- **Prioritize High-Interest Debt:** Focus on paying down high-interest debt, such as credit card balances, to reduce overall interest costs.
- **Avoid Unnecessary Debt:** Be cautious with borrowing and only take on debt that aligns with your financial goals and ability to repay

11. Continued Financial Education

- **Stay Informed:** Keep learning about personal finance, investment strategies, and money management to make informed financial decisions.
- **Seek Professional Advice:** Consult financial advisors or attend workshops to gain insights and improve your financial literacy.

By understanding and addressing these aspects of life after college, you can build a strong financial foundation, manage your resources effectively, and work towards achieving your longterm goals.

"Every smart financial choice in college is a step toward building a credit score you'll be proud of!"

PART NINE

Understanding and Monitoring Your Monthly Financial Activities

- Annual Credit Review
- 52 Week Saving Goals Challenge
- Credit Score Goals
- Credit Score Wheel
- Credit Score Tracker
- Credit Score Chart
- Student Loan Management
- Monthly Credit Review

Annual Credit Review

52-Week Savings Goal *Challenge*

Goal Amount

Week	Deposit	Balance	Done
1			☐
2			☐
3			☐
4			☐
5			☐
6			☐
7			☐
8			☐
9			☐
10			☐
11			☐
12			☐
13			☐
14			☐
15			☐
16			☐
17			☐
18			☐
19			☐
20			☐
21			☐
22			☐
23			☐
24			☐
25			☐
26			☐

Week	Deposit	Balance	Done
27			☐
28			☐
29			☐
30			☐
31			☐
32			☐
33			☐
34			☐
35			☐
36			☐
37			☐
38			☐
39			☐
40			☐
41			☐
42			☐
43			☐
44			☐
45			☐
46			☐
47			☐
48			☐
49			☐
50			☐
51			☐
52			☐

Credit Score *Goals*

YEAR: GOAL:

MY MONEY MANTRA OF THE YEAR

“

PRIORITIES

1	2	3

ACTION STEPS	ACTION STEPS	ACTION STEPS
1	1	1
2	2	2
3	3	3
4	4	4
5	5	5

NOTES

Credit Score *Wheel*

Monitor your credit score with this colorful monthly wheel tracker, transforming it into an enjoyable activity that helps you track progress and leads you on the path to financial success!

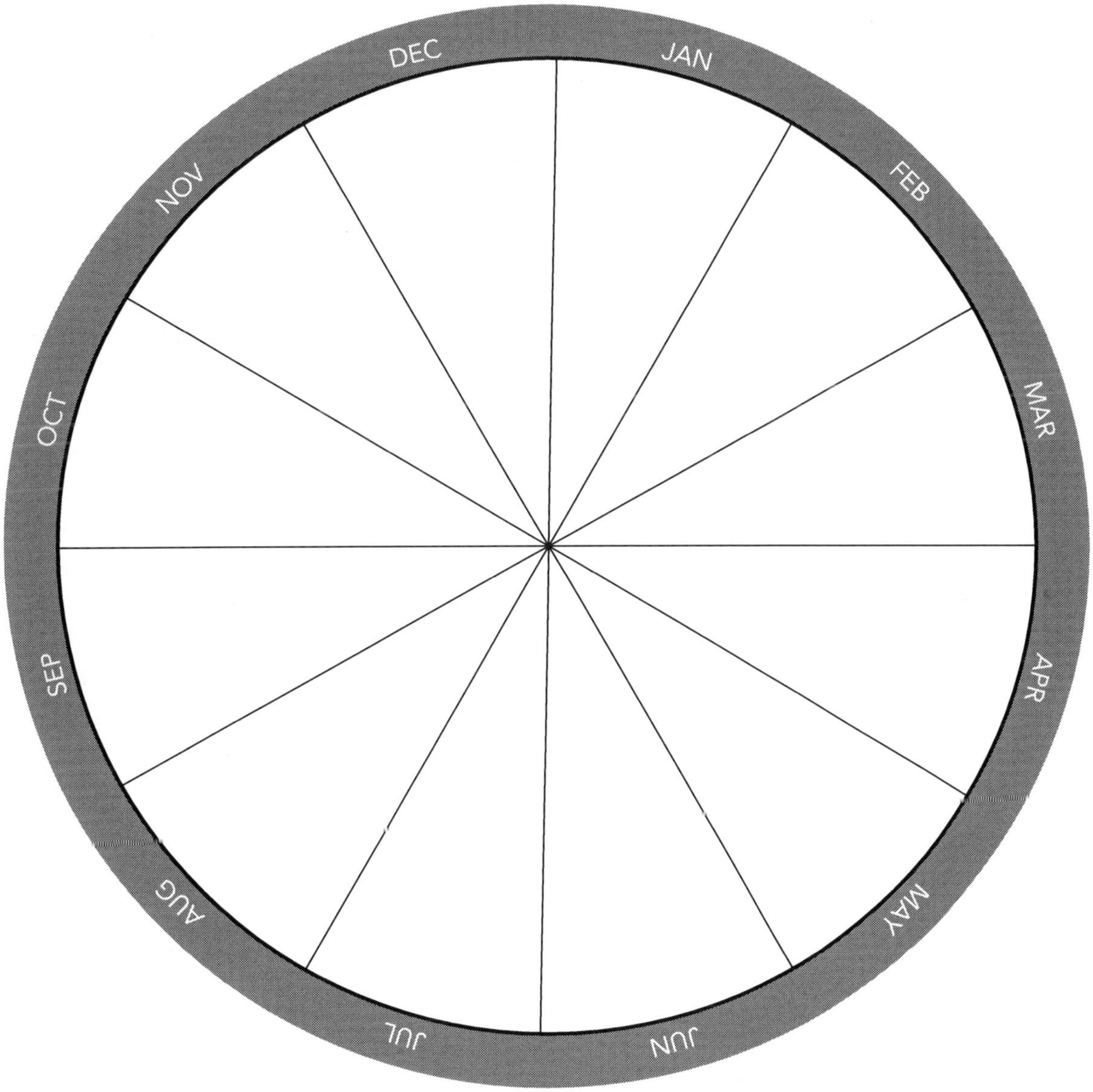

Credit Score Range	**Colors**
800-850 | Excellent	Dark Green
740-799 | Very Good	Light Green
670-739 | Good	Yellow
580-669 | Fair	Orange
300-579 | Poor	Red

Credit Score *Tracker*

YEAR: CURRENT SCORE: GOAL:

900
850
800
750
700
650
600
550
500
450
400
350
300

JAN FEB MAR APR MAY JUN JUL AUG SEP OCT NOV DEC

Q 1

JAN

FEB

MAR

Q 2

APR

MAY

JUN

Q 3

JUL

AUG

SEP

Q 4

OCT

NOV

DEC

Credit Score *Chart*

YEAR:

JANUARY	
TRANSUNION	
EQUIFAX	
EXPERIAN	

FEBRUARY	
TRANSUNION	
EQUIFAX	
EXPERIAN	

MARCH	
TRANSUNION	
EQUIFAX	
EXPERIAN	

APRIL	
TRANSUNION	
EQUIFAX	
EXPERIAN	

MAY	
TRANSUNION	
EQUIFAX	
EXPERIAN	

JUNE	
TRANSUNION	
EQUIFAX	
EXPERIAN	

JULY	
TRANSUNION	
EQUIFAX	
EXPERIAN	

AUGUST	
TRANSUNION	
EQUIFAX	
EXPERIAN	

SEPTEMBER	
TRANSUNION	
EQUIFAX	
EXPERIAN	

OCTOBER	
TRANSUNION	
EQUIFAX	
EXPERIAN	

NOVEMBER	
TRANSUNION	
EQUIFAX	
EXPERIAN	

DECEMBER	
TRANSUNION	
EQUIFAX	
EXPERIAN	

Student Loan *Management*

Personal Information

- **School Name:** ____________________
- **Graduation Date:** ____________________

LOAN INFORMATION

LOAN NAME	LENDER/ SERVICER	LOAN TYPE	PRINCIPAL AMOUNT	INTEREST RATE	REPAYMENT TERM	MONTHLY PAYMENT	DUE DATE	STATUS
1.								
2.								
3.								

Loan Summary

- **Total Principal Amount:** ____________________
- **Total Interest:** ____________________
- **Total Monthly Payment:** ____________________
- **Total Amount Paid to Date:** ____________________
- **Remaining Balance:** ____________________

Repayment Plan

- **Selected Repayment Plan:**
  (Standard, Graduated, Income-Driven, etc.) ____________________
- **Projected Payoff Date:** ____________________
- **Interest Savings:**
  (If using a repayment strategy like paying extra) ____________________

PAYMENT TRACKER

	PAYMENT DATE	PAYMENT AMOUNT	LOAN NAME	PAYMENT METHOD	BALANCE AFTER PAYMENT
JAN					
FEB					
MAR					
APR					
MAY					
JUN					
JUL					
AUG					
SEP					
OCT					
NOV					
DEC					

Payment Reminders

- **Next Payment Due Date:** ________________
- **Reminder Date:** ________________
- **Automatic Payments Setup:** ☐ Yes ☐ No

Forgiveness & Assistance Programs

- **Eligibility for Loan Forgiveness:**
(e.g., Public Service Loan Forgiveness) ____________________________
- **Application Status:** ____________________________
- **Next Steps:**

____

____

____

MONTHLY NOTES AND ACTION ITEMS

	NOTES	ACTION ITEMS
JAN		
FEB		
MAR		
APR		
MAY		
JUN		
JUL		
AUG		
SEP		
OCT		
NOV		
DEC		

Monthly Credit Review

January

SMART Financial Goals *Worksheet*

JAN ○ FEB ○ MAR ○ APR ○ MAY ○ JUN ○ JUL ○ AUG ○ SEP ○ OCT ○ NOV ○ DEC ○

Description of Goals					
SPECIFIC Cost					
MEASURABLE Monthly Amount					
ATTAINABLE Method/Steps					
REALISTIC Goal Length					
TIMEBOUND Your Timeline					

Notes

Monthly Budget *Planner*

JAN ○ FEB ○ MAR ○ APR ○ MAY ○ JUN ○ JUL ○ AUG ○ SEP ○ OCT ○ NOV ○ DEC ○

INCOME	AMOUNT
TOTAL	

BILLS	AMOUNT
TOTAL	

SAVINGS	AMOUNT
TOTAL	

EXPENSES	AMOUNT
TOTAL	

DEBT	AMOUNT
TOTAL	

SUMMARY	AMOUNT
INCOME	
BILLS	
SAVINGS	
EXPENSES	
DEBT	
TOTAL	

Bills Payment *Calendar*

JAN ○ FEB ○ MAR ○ APR ○ MAY ○ JUN ○ JUL ○ AUG ○ SEP ○ OCT ○ NOV ○ DEC ○

SUN	MON	TUE	WED	THU	FRI	SAT

Debt Repayment *Plan*

JAN ○ FEB ○ MAR ○ APR ○ MAY ○ JUN ○ JUL ○ AUG ○ SEP ○ OCT ○ NOV ○ DEC ○

Creditor:	Debt Type:
Starting Balance:	Credit Limit:
Repayment Frequency:	Interest Rate:
Goal Pay Off Date:	Min Repayment:

DATE	REPAYMENT	BALANCE	NOTES

Expense *Tracker*

JAN ○ FEB ○ MAR ○ APR ○ MAY ○ JUN ○ JUL ○ AUG ○ SEP ○ OCT ○ NOV ○ DEC ○

DATE	DESCRIPTION	AMOUNT	NOTES

TOTAL ____________________

Credit Card *Tracker*

JAN	FEB	MAR	APR	MAY	JUN	JUL	AUG	SEP	OCT	NOV	DEC
○	○	○	○	○	○	○	○	○	○	○	○

DATE	CREDIT CARD	CREDIT LIMIT	%RATE	AMOUNT DUE	AMOUNT PAID	BALANCE

Monthly Financial *Reflection*

JAN ○ FEB ○ MAR ○ APR ○ MAY ○ JUN ○ JUL ○ AUG ○ SEP ○ OCT ○ NOV ○ DEC ○

TOTAL INCOME	TOTAL EXPENSES	DIFFERENCE	BALANCE

Biggest Wins this Month

What am I grateful for?

What do I need to improve for next month?

What did I learn by tracking my finances this month?

Wish *List*

JAN ○ FEB ○ MAR ○ APR ○ MAY ○ JUN ○ JUL ○ AUG ○ SEP ○ OCT ○ NOV ○ DEC ○

WISH LIST	HOPE TO PAY	WHERE TO BUY	BOUGHT	SPENT	SAVED	NOTES
			☐			
			☐			
			☐			
			☐			
			☐			
			☐			
			☐			
			☐			
			☐			
			☐			
			☐			
			☐			
			☐			
			☐			
			☐			
			☐			
			☐			
			☐			
			☐			
			☐			
			☐			
			☐			
			☐			
			☐			

Emergency Fund *Tracker*

JAN ○ FEB ○ MAR ○ APR ○ MAY ○ JUN ○ JUL ○ AUG ○ SEP ○ OCT ○ NOV ○ DEC ○

AMOUNT NEEDED:	TARGET DATE:
MONTHLY SAVINGS TARGET:	ACCOUNT:

Progress Tracker

10%	20%	30%	40%	50%	60%	70%	80%	90%	100%

DATE	DEPOSIT	WITHDRAW	NOTES	BALANCE

Notes

Credit Networking and *Mentorship*

JAN ○ FEB ○ MAR ○ APR ○ MAY ○ JUN ○ JUL ○ AUG ○ SEP ○ OCT ○ NOV ○ DEC ○

Networking Goals

What specific goals do you have for networking this month?

1 ______________________________

2 ______________________________

3 ______________________________

Mentorship Goals

What do you want to achieve with the help of a mentor this month?

1 ______________________________

2 ______________________________

3 ______________________________

Identify Networking Opportunities

Events & Workshops

List credit-related events, workshops, or webinars to attend this month:

1 ______________________________

2 ______________________________

3 ______________________________

Online Communities

Identify online groups or forums where you can engage with others focused on credit improvement:

1 ____

2 ____

3 ____

Track Your Progress

Networking Activities

Record your networking activities for the month (e.g., events attended, new connections made):

1 ____

2 ____

3 ____

Mentorship Activities:

Record your interactions with mentors (e.g., meetings, advice received):

1 ____

2 ____

3 ____

Notes

____

____

____

Charity and *Giving*

JAN ○ FEB ○ MAR ○ APR ○ MAY ○ JUN ○ JUL ○ AUG ○ SEP ○ OCT ○ NOV ○ DEC ○

DONATION	ORGANIZATION	DATE GIVEN	VALUE	TAX DEDUCTIBLE

Self-care and Financial *Health*

JAN ○ FEB ○ MAR ○ APR ○ MAY ○ JUN ○ JUL ○ AUG ○ SEP ○ OCT ○ NOV ○ DEC ○

Self-Care Reflection

- **Physical Well-being**

  What physical health activities will you focus on this month?

  o ________________________________

  o ________________________________

- **Emotional & Mental Wellness**

  What mental health activities will you focus on this month?

  o ________________________________

  o ________________________________

- **Time for Self-Care**

  How will you make time for yourself?

  o ________________________________

  o ________________________________

Financial Health Reflection

- **Current Financial Practices**

  What financial habits do you want to maintain or improve this month?

  o ________________________________

  o ________________________________

- **Financial Goals**

  List your financial goals for this month

  - o ______________________________
  - o ______________________________

- **Financial Self-Care**

  How will you manage financial stress?

  - o ______________________________
  - o ______________________________

Accountability & Progress

- **Support System**

  Who will help you stay accountable this month?

  - o ______________________________
  - o ______________________________

- **Tracking Progress**

  How will you monitor your progress? (e.g., weekly check-ins, journaling)

  - o ______________________________
  - o ______________________________

- **End-of-Month Review Date**

  Set a date to review your goals and make any necessary adjustments

  - o ______________________________

February

SMART Financial Goals *Worksheet*

JAN ○ FEB ○ MAR ○ APR ○ MAY ○ JUN ○ JUL ○ AUG ○ SEP ○ OCT ○ NOV ○ DEC ○

Description of Goals					
SPECIFIC Cost					
MEASURABLE Monthly Amount					
ATTAINABLE Method/Steps					
REALISTIC Goal Length					
TIMEBOUND Your Timeline					

Notes

Monthly Budget *Planner*

JAN ○ FEB ○ MAR ○ APR ○ MAY ○ JUN ○ JUL ○ AUG ○ SEP ○ OCT ○ NOV ○ DEC ○

INCOME	AMOUNT
TOTAL	

BILLS	AMOUNT
TOTAL	

SAVINGS	AMOUNT
TOTAL	

EXPENSES	AMOUNT
TOTAL	

DEBT	AMOUNT
TOTAL	

SUMMARY	AMOUNT
INCOME	
BILLS	
SAVINGS	
EXPENSES	
DEBT	
TOTAL	

Bills Payment *Calendar*

JAN ○ FEB ○ MAR ○ APR ○ MAY ○ JUN ○ JUL ○ AUG ○ SEP ○ OCT ○ NOV ○ DEC ○

SUN	MON	TUE	WED	THU	FRI	SAT

Debt Repayment *Plan*

JAN	FEB	MAR	APR	MAY	JUN	JUL	AUG	SEP	OCT	NOV	DEC
○	○	○	○	○	○	○	○	○	○	○	○

Creditor:	Debt Type:
Starting Balance:	Credit Limit:
Repayment Frequency:	Interest Rate:
Goal Pay Off Date:	Min Repayment:

DATE	REPAYMENT	BALANCE	NOTES

Expense *Tracker*

JAN ○ FEB ○ MAR ○ APR ○ MAY ○ JUN ○ JUL ○ AUG ○ SEP ○ OCT ○ NOV ○ DEC ○

DATE	DESCRIPTION	AMOUNT	NOTES

TOTAL ______________________

Credit Card *Tracker*

JAN ○ FEB ○ MAR ○ APR ○ MAY ○ JUN ○ JUL ○ AUG ○ SEP ○ OCT ○ NOV ○ DEC ○

DATE	CREDIT CARD	CREDIT LIMIT	%RATE	AMOUNT DUE	AMOUNT PAID	BALANCE

Monthly Financial *Reflection*

JAN ○ FEB ○ MAR ○ APR ○ MAY ○ JUN ○ JUL ○ AUG ○ SEP ○ OCT ○ NOV ○ DEC ○

TOTAL INCOME	TOTAL EXPENSES	DIFFERENCE	BALANCE

Biggest Wins this Month

What am I grateful for?

What do I need to improve for next month?

What did I learn by tracking my finances this month?

Wish *List*

JAN ○ FEB ○ MAR ○ APR ○ MAY ○ JUN ○ JUL ○ AUG ○ SEP ○ OCT ○ NOV ○ DEC ○

WISH LIST	HOPE TO PAY	WHERE TO BUY	BOUGHT	SPENT	SAVED	NOTES
			☐			
			☐			
			☐			
			☐			
			☐			
			☐			
			☐			
			☐			
			☐			
			☐			
			☐			
			☐			
			☐			
			☐			
			☐			
			☐			
			☐			
			☐			
			☐			
			☐			
			☐			
			☐			
			☐			
			☐			

Emergency Fund *Tracker*

JAN ○ FEB ○ MAR ○ APR ○ MAY ○ JUN ○ JUL ○ AUG ○ SEP ○ OCT ○ NOV ○ DEC ○

AMOUNT NEEDED:	TARGET DATE:
MONTHLY SAVINGS TARGET:	ACCOUNT:

Progress Tracker

10%	20%	30%	40%	50%	60%	70%	80%	90%	100%

DATE	DEPOSIT	WITHDRAW	NOTES	BALANCE

Notes

Credit Networking and *Mentorship*

JAN ○ FEB ○ MAR ○ APR ○ MAY ○ JUN ○ JUL ○ AUG ○ SEP ○ OCT ○ NOV ○ DEC ○

Networking Goals

What specific goals do you have for networking this month?

1 ____

2 ____

3 ____

Mentorship Goals

What do you want to achieve with the help of a mentor this month?

1 ____

2 ____

3 ____

Identify Networking Opportunities

Events & Workshops

List credit-related events, workshops, or webinars to attend this month:

1 ____

2 ____

3 ____

Online Communities

Identify online groups or forums where you can engage with others focused on credit improvement:

1 ______________________________

2 ______________________________

3 ______________________________

Track Your Progress

Networking Activities

Record your networking activities for the month (e.g., events attended, new connections made):

1 ______________________________

2 ______________________________

3 ______________________________

Mentorship Activities:

Record your interactions with mentors (e.g., meetings, advice received).

1 ______________________________

2 ______________________________

3 ______________________________

Notes

____

____

____

Charity and *Giving*

JAN	FEB	MAR	APR	MAY	JUN	JUL	AUG	SEP	OCT	NOV	DEC
○	○	○	○	○	○	○	○	○	○	○	○

DONATION	ORGANIZATION	DATE GIVEN	VALUE	TAX DEDUCTIBLE

Self-care and Financial *Health*

JAN ○ FEB ○ MAR ○ APR ○ MAY ○ JUN ○ JUL ○ AUG ○ SEP ○ OCT ○ NOV ○ DEC ○

Self-Care Reflection

- **Physical Well-being**

  What physical health activities will you focus on this month?

  o ______________________________

  o ______________________________

- **Emotional & Mental Wellness**

  What mental health activities will you focus on this month?

  o ______________________________

  o ______________________________

- **Time for Self-Care**

  How will you make time for yourself?

  o ______________________________

  o ______________________________

Financial Health Reflection

- **Current Financial Practices**

  What financial habits do you want to maintain or improve this month?

  o ______________________________

  o ______________________________

- **Financial Goals**

  List your financial goals for this month

  o ______________________________

  o ______________________________

- **Financial Self-Care**

  How will you manage financial stress?

  o ______________________________

  o ______________________________

Accountability & Progress

- **Support System**

  Who will help you stay accountable this month?

  o ______________________________

  o ______________________________

- **Tracking Progress**

  How will you monitor your progress? (e.g., weekly check-ins, journaling)

  o ______________________________

  o ______________________________

- **End-of-Month Review Date**

  Set a date to review your goals and make any necessary adjustments

  o ______________________________

March

SMART Financial Goals *Worksheet*

JAN ○ FEB ○ MAR ○ APR ○ MAY ○ JUN ○ JUL ○ AUG ○ SEP ○ OCT ○ NOV ○ DEC ○

Description of Goals					
SPECIFIC Cost					
MEASURABLE Monthly Amount					
ATTAINABLE Method/Steps					
REALISTIC Goal Length					
TIMEBOUND Your Timeline					

Notes

Monthly Budget *Planner*

JAN ○ FEB ○ MAR ○ APR ○ MAY ○ JUN ○ JUL ○ AUG ○ SEP ○ OCT ○ NOV ○ DEC ○

INCOME	AMOUNT
TOTAL	

BILLS	AMOUNT
TOTAL	

SAVINGS	AMOUNT
TOTAL	

EXPENSES	AMOUNT
TOTAL	

DEBT	AMOUNT
TOTAL	

SUMMARY	AMOUNT
INCOME	
BILLS	
SAVINGS	
EXPENSES	
DEBT	
TOTAL	

Bills Payment *Calendar*

JAN ○ FEB ○ MAR ○ APR ○ MAY ○ JUN ○ JUL ○ AUG ○ SEP ○ OCT ○ NOV ○ DEC ○

SUN	MON	TUE	WED	THU	FRI	SAT
○ ○	○ ○	○ ○	○ ○	○ ○	○ ○	○ ○
○ ○	○ ○	○ ○	○ ○	○ ○	○ ○	○ ○
○ ○	○ ○	○ ○	○ ○	○ ○	○ ○	○ ○
○ ○	○ ○	○ ○	○ ○	○ ○	○ ○	○ ○
○ ○	○ ○	○ ○	○ ○	○ ○	○ ○	○ ○

Debt Repayment *Plan*

JAN	FEB	MAR	APR	MAY	JUN	JUL	AUG	SEP	OCT	NOV	DEC
○	○	○	○	○	○	○	○	○	○	○	○

Creditor:	Debt Type:
Starting Balance:	Credit Limit:
Repayment Frequency:	Interest Rate:
Goal Pay Off Date:	Min Repayment:

DATE	REPAYMENT	BALANCE	NOTES

Expense *Tracker*

JAN ○ FEB ○ MAR ○ APR ○ MAY ○ JUN ○ JUL ○ AUG ○ SEP ○ OCT ○ NOV ○ DEC ○

DATE	DESCRIPTION	AMOUNT	NOTES

TOTAL ____________________

Credit Card *Tracker*

JAN ○ FEB ○ MAR ○ APR ○ MAY ○ JUN ○ JUL ○ AUG ○ SEP ○ OCT ○ NOV ○ DEC ○

DATE	CREDIT CARD	CREDIT LIMIT	%RATE	AMOUNT DUE	AMOUNT PAID	BALANCE

Monthly Financial *Reflection*

JAN ○ FEB ○ MAR ○ APR ○ MAY ○ JUN ○ JUL ○ AUG ○ SEP ○ OCT ○ NOV ○ DEC ○

TOTAL INCOME	TOTAL EXPENSES	DIFFERENCE	BALANCE

Biggest Wins this Month

What am I grateful for?

What do I need to improve for next month?

What did I learn by tracking my finances this month?

Wish *List*

JAN ○ FEB ○ MAR ○ APR ○ MAY ○ JUN ○ JUL ○ AUG ○ SEP ○ OCT ○ NOV ○ DEC ○

WISH LIST	HOPE TO PAY	WHERE TO BUY	BOUGHT	SPENT	SAVED	NOTES
			☐			
			☐			
			☐			
			☐			
			☐			
			☐			
			☐			
			☐			
			☐			
			☐			
			☐			
			☐			
			☐			
			☐			
			☐			
			☐			
			☐			
			☐			
			☐			
			☐			
			☐			
			☐			
			☐			
			☐			

Emergency Fund *Tracker*

JAN ○ FEB ○ MAR ○ APR ○ MAY ○ JUN ○ JUL ○ AUG ○ SEP ○ OCT ○ NOV ○ DEC ○

AMOUNT NEEDED:	TARGET DATE:
MONTHLY SAVINGS TARGET:	ACCOUNT:

Progress Tracker

10%	20%	30%	40%	50%	60%	70%	80%	90%	100%

DATE	DEPOSIT	WITHDRAW	NOTES	BALANCE

Notes

Credit Networking and *Mentorship*

JAN ○ FEB ○ MAR ○ APR ○ MAY ○ JUN ○ JUL ○ AUG ○ SEP ○ OCT ○ NOV ○ DEC ○

Networking Goals

What specific goals do you have for networking this month?

1 ____

2 ____

3 ____

Mentorship Goals

What do you want to achieve with the help of a mentor this month?

1 ____

2 ____

3 ____

Identify Networking Opportunities

Events & Workshops

List credit-related events, workshops, or webinars to attend this month:

1 ____

2 ____

3 ____

Online Communities

Identify online groups or forums where you can engage with others focused on credit improvement:

1 ___

2 ___

3 ___

Track Your Progress

Networking Activities

Record your networking activities for the month (e.g., events attended, new connections made):

1 ___

2 ___

3 ___

Mentorship Activities:

Record your interactions with mentors (e.g., meetings, advice received):

1 ___

2 ___

3 ___

Notes

Charity and *Giving*

JAN ○ FEB ○ MAR ○ APR ○ MAY ○ JUN ○ JUL ○ AUG ○ SEP ○ OCT ○ NOV ○ DEC ○

DONATION	ORGANIZATION	DATE GIVEN	VALUE	TAX DEDUCTIBLE

Self-care and Financial *Health*

JAN ○ FEB ○ MAR ○ APR ○ MAY ○ JUN ○ JUL ○ AUG ○ SEP ○ OCT ○ NOV ○ DEC ○

Self-Care Reflection

- **Physical Well-being**

  What physical health activities will you focus on this month?

  - ○ ______
  - ○ ______

- **Emotional & Mental Wellness**

  What mental health activities will you focus on this month?

  - ○ ______
  - ○ ______

- **Time for Self-Care**

  How will you make time for yourself?

  - ○ ______
  - ○ ______

Financial Health Reflection

- **Current Financial Practices**

  What financial habits do you want to maintain or improve this month?

  - ○ ______
  - ○ ______

- **Financial Goals**

  List your financial goals for this month

  o ______________________________

  o ______________________________

- **Financial Self-Care**

  How will you manage financial stress?

  o ______________________________

  o ______________________________

Accountability & Progress

- **Support System**

  Who will help you stay accountable this month?

  o ______________________________

  o ______________________________

- **Tracking Progress**

  How will you monitor your progress? (e.g., weekly check-ins, journaling)

  o ______________________________

  o ______________________________

- **End-of-Month Review Date**

  Set a date to review your goals and make any necessary adjustments

  o ______________________________

April

SMART Financial Goals *Worksheet*

JAN ○ FEB ○ MAR ○ APR ○ MAY ○ JUN ○ JUL ○ AUG ○ SEP ○ OCT ○ NOV ○ DEC ○

Description of Goals					
SPECIFIC Cost					
MEASURABLE Monthly Amount					
ATTAINABLE Method/Steps					
REALISTIC Goal Length					
TIMEBOUND Your Timeline					

Notes

Monthly Budget *Planner*

JAN ○ FEB ○ MAR ○ APR ○ MAY ○ JUN ○ JUL ○ AUG ○ SEP ○ OCT ○ NOV ○ DEC ○

INCOME	AMOUNT
TOTAL	

EXPENSES	AMOUNT
TOTAL	

BILLS	AMOUNT
TOTAL	

DEBT	AMOUNT
TOTAL	

SAVINGS	AMOUNT
TOTAL	

SUMMARY	AMOUNT
INCOME	
BILLS	
SAVINGS	
EXPENSES	
DEBT	
TOTAL	

Bills Payment *Calendar*

JAN ○ FEB ○ MAR ○ APR ○ MAY ○ JUN ○ JUL ○ AUG ○ SEP ○ OCT ○ NOV ○ DEC ○

SUN	MON	TUE	WED	THU	FRI	SAT
○ ___ ○ ___	○ ___ ○ ___	○ ___ ○ ___	○ ___ ○ ___	○ ___ ○ ___	○ ___ ○ ___	○ ___ ○ ___
○ ___ ○ ___	○ ___ ○ ___	○ ___ ○ ___	○ ___ ○ ___	○ ___ ○ ___	○ ___ ○ ___	○ ___ ○ ___
○ ___ ○ ___	○ ___ ○ ___	○ ___ ○ ___	○ ___ ○ ___	○ ___ ○ ___	○ ___ ○ ___	○ ___ ○ ___
○ ___ ○ ___	○ ___ ○ ___	○ ___ ○ ___	○ ___ ○ ___	○ ___ ○ ___	○ ___ ○ ___	○ ___ ○ ___
○ ___ ○ ___	○ ___ ○ ___	○ ___ ○ ___	○ ___ ○ ___	○ ___ ○ ___	○ ___ ○ ___	○ ___ ○ ___

Debt Repayment *Plan*

JAN	FEB	MAR	APR	MAY	JUN	JUL	AUG	SEP	OCT	NOV	DEC
○	○	○	○	○	○	○	○	○	○	○	○

Creditor:	Debt Type:
Starting Balance:	Credit Limit:
Repayment Frequency:	Interest Rate:
Goal Pay Off Date:	Min Repayment:

DATE	REPAYMENT	BALANCE	NOTES

Expense *Tracker*

JAN ○ FEB ○ MAR ○ APR ○ MAY ○ JUN ○ JUL ○ AUG ○ SEP ○ OCT ○ NOV ○ DEC ○

DATE	DESCRIPTION	AMOUNT	NOTES

TOTAL ______________________

Credit Card *Tracker*

JAN ○ FEB ○ MAR ○ APR ○ MAY ○ JUN ○ JUL ○ AUG ○ SEP ○ OCT ○ NOV ○ DEC ○

DATE	CREDIT CARD	CREDIT LIMIT	%RATE	AMOUNT DUE	AMOUNT PAID	BALANCE

Monthly Financial *Reflection*

JAN ○ FEB ○ MAR ○ APR ○ MAY ○ JUN ○ JUL ○ AUG ○ SEP ○ OCT ○ NOV ○ DEC ○

TOTAL INCOME	TOTAL EXPENSES	DIFFERENCE	BALANCE

Biggest Wins this Month

What am I grateful for?

What do I need to improve for next month?

What did I learn by tracking my finances this month?

Wish *List*

JAN ○ FEB ○ MAR ○ APR ○ MAY ○ JUN ○ JUL ○ AUG ○ SEP ○ OCT ○ NOV ○ DEC ○

WISH LIST	HOPE TO PAY	WHERE TO BUY	BOUGHT	SPENT	SAVED	NOTES
			☐			
			☐			
			☐			
			☐			
			☐			
			☐			
			☐			
			☐			
			☐			
			☐			
			☐			
			☐			
			☐			
			☐			
			☐			
			☐			
			☐			
			☐			
			☐			
			☐			
			☐			
			☐			
			☐			
			☐			

Emergency Fund *Tracker*

JAN ○ FEB ○ MAR ○ APR ○ MAY ○ JUN ○ JUL ○ AUG ○ SEP ○ OCT ○ NOV ○ DEC ○

AMOUNT NEEDED:	TARGET DATE:
MONTHLY SAVINGS TARGET:	ACCOUNT:

Progress Tracker

10%	20%	30%	40%	50%	60%	70%	80%	90%	100%

DATE	DEPOSIT	WITHDRAW	NOTES	BALANCE

Notes

Credit Networking and *Mentorship*

JAN ○ FEB ○ MAR ○ APR ○ MAY ○ JUN ○ JUL ○ AUG ○ SEP ○ OCT ○ NOV ○ DEC ○

Networking Goals

What specific goals do you have for networking this month?

1 ____________________

2 ____________________

3 ____________________

Mentorship Goals

What do you want to achieve with the help of a mentor this month?

1 ____________________

2 ____________________

3 ____________________

Identify Networking Opportunities

Events & Workshops

List credit-related events, workshops, or webinars to attend this month:

1 ____________________

2 ____________________

3 ____________________

Online Communities

Identify online groups or forums where you can engage with others focused on credit improvement:

1 ________________________________

2 ________________________________

3 ________________________________

Track Your Progress

Networking Activities

Record your networking activities for the month (e.g., events attended, new connections made):

1 ________________________________

2 ________________________________

3 ________________________________

Mentorship Activities:

Record your interactions with mentors (e.g., meetings, advice received).

1 ________________________________

2 ________________________________

3 ________________________________

Notes

Charity and *Giving*

JAN ○ FEB ○ MAR ○ APR ○ MAY ○ JUN ○ JUL ○ AUG ○ SEP ○ OCT ○ NOV ○ DEC ○

DONATION	ORGANIZATION	DATE GIVEN	VALUE	TAX DEDUCTIBLE

Self-care and Financial *Health*

JAN ○ FEB ○ MAR ○ APR ○ MAY ○ JUN ○ JUL ○ AUG ○ SEP ○ OCT ○ NOV ○ DEC ○

Self-Care Reflection

- **Physical Well-being**

  What physical health activities will you focus on this month?

  - o ______________________________
  - o ______________________________

- **Emotional & Mental Wellness**

  What mental health activities will you focus on this month?

  - o ______________________________
  - o ______________________________

- **Time for Self-Care**

  How will you make time for yourself?

  - o ______________________________
  - o ______________________________

Financial Health Reflection

- **Current Financial Practices**

  What financial habits do you want to maintain or improve this month?

  - o ______________________________
  - o ______________________________

- **Financial Goals**

  List your financial goals for this month

  - o ______________________________
  - o ______________________________

- **Financial Self-Care**

  How will you manage financial stress?

  - o ______________________________
  - o ______________________________

Accountability & Progress

- **Support System**

  Who will help you stay accountable this month?

  - o ______________________________
  - o ______________________________

- **Tracking Progress**

  How will you monitor your progress? (e.g., weekly check-ins, journaling)

  - o ______________________________
  - o ______________________________

- **End-of-Month Review Date**

  Set a date to review your goals and make any necessary adjustments

  - o ______________________________

May

SMART Financial Goals *Worksheet*

JAN ○ FEB ○ MAR ○ APR ○ MAY ○ JUN ○ JUL ○ AUG ○ SEP ○ OCT ○ NOV ○ DEC ○

Description of Goals					
SPECIFIC Cost					
MEASURABLE Monthly Amount					
ATTAINABLE Method/Steps					
REALISTIC Goal Length					
TIMEBOUND Your Timeline					

Notes

Monthly Budget *Planner*

JAN ○ FEB ○ MAR ○ APR ○ MAY ○ JUN ○ JUL ○ AUG ○ SEP ○ OCT ○ NOV ○ DEC ○

INCOME	AMOUNT
TOTAL	

BILLS	AMOUNT
TOTAL	

SAVINGS	AMOUNT
TOTAL	

EXPENSES	AMOUNT
TOTAL	

DEBT	AMOUNT
TOTAL	

SUMMARY	AMOUNT
INCOME	
BILLS	
SAVINGS	
EXPENSES	
DEBT	
TOTAL	

Bills Payment *Calendar*

JAN ○ FEB ○ MAR ○ APR ○ MAY ○ JUN ○ JUL ○ AUG ○ SEP ○ OCT ○ NOV ○ DEC ○

SUN	MON	TUE	WED	THU	FRI	SAT
○ ○	○ ○	○ ○	○ ○	○ ○	○ ○	○ ○
○ ○	○ ○	○ ○	○ ○	○ ○	○ ○	○ ○
○ ○	○ ○	○ ○	○ ○	○ ○	○ ○	○ ○
○ ○	○ ○	○ ○	○ ○	○ ○	○ ○	○ ○
○ ○	○ ○	○ ○	○ ○	○ ○	○ ○	○ ○

Debt Repayment *Plan*

JAN ○ FEB ○ MAR ○ APR ○ MAY ○ JUN ○ JUL ○ AUG ○ SEP ○ OCT ○ NOV ○ DEC ○

Creditor:	Debt Type:
Starting Balance:	Credit Limit:
Repayment Frequency:	Interest Rate:
Goal Pay Off Date:	Min Repayment:

DATE	REPAYMENT	BALANCE	NOTES

Expense *Tracker*

JAN ○ FEB ○ MAR ○ APR ○ MAY ○ JUN ○ JUL ○ AUG ○ SEP ○ OCT ○ NOV ○ DEC ○

DATE	DESCRIPTION	AMOUNT	NOTES

TOTAL ______________________

Credit Card *Tracker*

JAN ○ FEB ○ MAR ○ APR ○ MAY ○ JUN ○ JUL ○ AUG ○ SEP ○ OCT ○ NOV ○ DEC ○

DATE	CREDIT CARD	CREDIT LIMIT	%RATE	AMOUNT DUE	AMOUNT PAID	BALANCE

Monthly Financial *Reflection*

JAN ○ FEB ○ MAR ○ APR ○ MAY ○ JUN ○ JUL ○ AUG ○ SEP ○ OCT ○ NOV ○ DEC ○

TOTAL INCOME	TOTAL EXPENSES	DIFFERENCE	BALANCE

Biggest Wins this Month

What am I grateful for?

What do I need to improve for next month?

What did I learn by tracking my finances this month?

Wish List

JAN ○ FEB ○ MAR ○ APR ○ MAY ○ JUN ○ JUL ○ AUG ○ SEP ○ OCT ○ NOV ○ DEC ○

WISH LIST	HOPE TO PAY	WHERE TO BUY	BOUGHT	SPENT	SAVED	NOTES
			☐			
			☐			
			☐			
			☐			
			☐			
			☐			
			☐			
			☐			
			☐			
			☐			
			☐			
			☐			
			☐			
			☐			
			☐			
			☐			
			☐			
			☐			
			☐			
			☐			
			☐			
			☐			
			☐			
			☐			

Emergency Fund *Tracker*

JAN	FEB	MAR	APR	MAY	JUN	JUL	AUG	SEP	OCT	NOV	DEC
○	○	○	○	○	○	○	○	○	○	○	○

AMOUNT NEEDED:	TARGET DATE:
MONTHLY SAVINGS TARGET:	ACCOUNT:

Progress Tracker

10%	20%	30%	40%	50%	60%	70%	80%	90%	100%

DATE	DEPOSIT	WITHDRAW	NOTES	BALANCE

Notes

Credit Networking and *Mentorship*

JAN ○ FEB ○ MAR ○ APR ○ MAY ○ JUN ○ JUL ○ AUG ○ SEP ○ OCT ○ NOV ○ DEC ○

Networking Goals

What specific goals do you have for networking this month?

1 ______________________________

2 ______________________________

3 ______________________________

Mentorship Goals

What do you want to achieve with the help of a mentor this month?

1 ______________________________

2 ______________________________

3 ______________________________

Identify Networking Opportunities

Events & Workshops

List credit-related events, workshops, or webinars to attend this month:

1 ______________________________

2 ______________________________

3 ______________________________

Online Communities

Identify online groups or forums where you can engage with others focused on credit improvement:

1 ____

2 ____

3 ____

Track Your Progress

Networking Activities

Record your networking activities for the month (e.g., events attended, new connections made):

1 ____

2 ____

3 ____

Mentorship Activities:

Record your interactions with mentors (e.g., meetings, advice received):

1 ____

2 ____

3 ____

Notes

Charity and *Giving*

JAN ○ FEB ○ MAR ○ APR ○ MAY ○ JUN ○ JUL ○ AUG ○ SEP ○ OCT ○ NOV ○ DEC ○

DONATION	ORGANIZATION	DATE GIVEN	VALUE	TAX DEDUCTIBLE

Self-care and Financial *Health*

JAN ○ FEB ○ MAR ○ APR ○ MAY ○ JUN ○ JUL ○ AUG ○ SEP ○ OCT ○ NOV ○ DEC ○

Self-Care Reflection

- **Physical Well-being**

  What physical health activities will you focus on this month?

  o ____________________

  o ____________________

- **Emotional & Mental Wellness**

  What mental health activities will you focus on this month?

  o ____________________

  o ____________________

- **Time for Self-Care**

  How will you make time for yourself?

  o ____________________

  o ____________________

Financial Health Reflection

- **Current Financial Practices**

  What financial habits do you want to maintain or improve this month?

  o ____________________

  o ____________________

- **Financial Goals**

  List your financial goals for this month

  - o ______________________________
  - o ______________________________

- **Financial Self-Care**

  How will you manage financial stress?

  - o ______________________________
  - o ______________________________

Accountability & Progress

- **Support System**

  Who will help you stay accountable this month?

  - o ______________________________
  - o ______________________________

- **Tracking Progress**

  How will you monitor your progress? (e.g., weekly check-ins, journaling)

  - o ______________________________
  - o ______________________________

- **End-of-Month Review Date**

  Set a date to review your goals and make any necessary adjustments

  - o ______________________________

June

SMART Financial Goals *Worksheet*

JAN ○ FEB ○ MAR ○ APR ○ MAY ○ JUN ○ JUL ○ AUG ○ SEP ○ OCT ○ NOV ○ DEC ○

Description of Goals					
SPECIFIC Cost					
MEASURABLE Monthly Amount					
ATTAINABLE Method/Steps					
REALISTIC Goal Length					
TIMEBOUND Your Timeline					

Notes

Monthly Budget *Planner*

JAN ○ FEB ○ MAR ○ APR ○ MAY ○ JUN ○ JUL ○ AUG ○ SEP ○ OCT ○ NOV ○ DEC ○

INCOME	AMOUNT
TOTAL	

BILLS	AMOUNT
TOTAL	

SAVINGS	AMOUNT
TOTAL	

EXPENSES	AMOUNT
TOTAL	

DEBT	AMOUNT
TOTAL	

SUMMARY	AMOUNT
INCOME	
BILLS	
SAVINGS	
EXPENSES	
DEBT	
TOTAL	

Bills Payment *Calendar*

JAN ○ FEB ○ MAR ○ APR ○ MAY ○ JUN ○ JUL ○ AUG ○ SEP ○ OCT ○ NOV ○ DEC ○

SUN	MON	TUE	WED	THU	FRI	SAT
○ ○	○ ○	○ ○	○ ○	○ ○	○ ○	○ ○
○ ○	○ ○	○ ○	○ ○	○ ○	○ ○	○ ○
○ ○	○ ○	○ ○	○ ○	○ ○	○ ○	○ ○
○ ○	○ ○	○ ○	○ ○	○ ○	○ ○	○ ○
○ ○	○ ○	○ ○	○ ○	○ ○	○ ○	○ ○

Debt Repayment *Plan*

JAN	FEB	MAR	APR	MAY	JUN	JUL	AUG	SEP	OCT	NOV	DEC
○	○	○	○	○	○	○	○	○	○	○	○

Creditor:	Debt Type:
Starting Balance:	Credit Limit:
Repayment Frequency:	Interest Rate:
Goal Pay Off Date:	Min Repayment:

DATE	REPAYMENT	BALANCE	NOTES

Expense *Tracker*

JAN ○ FEB ○ MAR ○ APR ○ MAY ○ JUN ○ JUL ○ AUG ○ SEP ○ OCT ○ NOV ○ DEC ○

DATE	DESCRIPTION	AMOUNT	NOTES

TOTAL ______________________

Credit Card *Tracker*

JAN ○ FEB ○ MAR ○ APR ○ MAY ○ JUN ○ JUL ○ AUG ○ SEP ○ OCT ○ NOV ○ DEC ○

DATE	CREDIT CARD	CREDIT LIMIT	%RATE	AMOUNT DUE	AMOUNT PAID	BALANCE

Monthly Financial *Reflection*

JAN ○ FEB ○ MAR ○ APR ○ MAY ○ JUN ○ JUL ○ AUG ○ SEP ○ OCT ○ NOV ○ DEC ○

TOTAL INCOME	TOTAL EXPENSES	DIFFERENCE	BALANCE

Biggest Wins this Month

What am I grateful for?

What do I need to improve for next month?

What did I learn by tracking my finances this month?

Wish *List*

JAN ○ FEB ○ MAR ○ APR ○ MAY ○ JUN ○ JUL ○ AUG ○ SEP ○ OCT ○ NOV ○ DEC ○

WISH LIST	HOPE TO PAY	WHERE TO BUY	BOUGHT	SPENT	SAVED	NOTES
			☐			
			☐			
			☐			
			☐			
			☐			
			☐			
			☐			
			☐			
			☐			
			☐			
			☐			
			☐			
			☐			
			☐			
			☐			
			☐			
			☐			
			☐			
			☐			
			☐			
			☐			
			☐			
			☐			
			☐			

Emergency Fund *Tracker*

JAN ○ FEB ○ MAR ○ APR ○ MAY ○ JUN ○ JUL ○ AUG ○ SEP ○ OCT ○ NOV ○ DEC ○

AMOUNT NEEDED:	TARGET DATE:
MONTHLY SAVINGS TARGET:	ACCOUNT:

Progress Tracker

10%	20%	30%	40%	50%	60%	70%	80%	90%	100%

DATE	DEPOSIT	WITHDRAW	NOTES	BALANCE

Notes

Credit Networking and *Mentorship*

JAN ○ FEB ○ MAR ○ APR ○ MAY ○ JUN ○ JUL ○ AUG ○ SEP ○ OCT ○ NOV ○ DEC ○

Networking Goals

What specific goals do you have for networking this month?

1 ______________________________

2 ______________________________

3 ______________________________

Mentorship Goals

What do you want to achieve with the help of a mentor this month?

1 ______________________________

2 ______________________________

3 ______________________________

Identify Networking Opportunities

Events & Workshops

List credit-related events, workshops, or webinars to attend this month:

1 ______________________________

2 ______________________________

3 ______________________________

Online Communities

Identify online groups or forums where you can engage with others focused on credit improvement:

1 ________________________________

2 ________________________________

3 ________________________________

Track Your Progress

Networking Activities

Record your networking activities for the month (e.g., events attended, new connections made):

1 ________________________________

2 ________________________________

3 ________________________________

Mentorship Activities:

Record your interactions with mentors (e.g., meetings, advice received):

1 ________________________________

2 ________________________________

3 ________________________________

Notes

____

____

____

Charity and *Giving*

JAN ○ FEB ○ MAR ○ APR ○ MAY ○ JUN ○ JUL ○ AUG ○ SEP ○ OCT ○ NOV ○ DEC ○

DONATION	ORGANIZATION	DATE GIVEN	VALUE	TAX DEDUCTIBLE

Self-care and Financial *Health*

JAN ○ FEB ○ MAR ○ APR ○ MAY ○ JUN ○ JUL ○ AUG ○ SEP ○ OCT ○ NOV ○ DEC ○

Self-Care Reflection

- **Physical Well-being**

  What physical health activities will you focus on this month?

  o ______________________________

  o ______________________________

- **Emotional & Mental Wellness**

  What mental health activities will you focus on this month?

  o ______________________________

  o ______________________________

- **Time for Self-Care**

  How will you make time for yourself?

  o ______________________________

  o ______________________________

Financial Health Reflection

- **Current Financial Practices**

  What financial habits do you want to maintain or improve this month?

  o ______________________________

  o ______________________________

- **Financial Goals**

  List your financial goals for this month

  o ______________________________

  o ______________________________

- **Financial Self-Care**

  How will you manage financial stress?

  o ______________________________

  o ______________________________

Accountability & Progress

- **Support System**

  Who will help you stay accountable this month?

  o ______________________________

  o ______________________________

- **Tracking Progress**

  How will you monitor your progress? (e.g., weekly check-ins, journaling)

  o ______________________________

  o ______________________________

- **End-of-Month Review Date**

  Set a date to review your goals and make any necessary adjustments

  o ______________________________

July

SMART Financial Goals *Worksheet*

JAN ○ FEB ○ MAR ○ APR ○ MAY ○ JUN ○ JUL ○ AUG ○ SEP ○ OCT ○ NOV ○ DEC ○

Description of Goals					
SPECIFIC Cost					
MEASURABLE Monthly Amount					
ATTAINABLE Method/Steps					
REALISTIC Goal Length					
TIMEBOUND Your Timeline					

Notes

Monthly Budget *Planner*

JAN ○ FEB ○ MAR ○ APR ○ MAY ○ JUN ○ JUL ○ AUG ○ SEP ○ OCT ○ NOV ○ DEC ○

INCOME	AMOUNT
TOTAL	

BILLS	AMOUNT
TOTAL	

SAVINGS	AMOUNT
TOTAL	

EXPENSES	AMOUNT
TOTAL	

DEBT	AMOUNT
TOTAL	

SUMMARY	AMOUNT
INCOME	
BILLS	
SAVINGS	
EXPENSES	
DEBT	
TOTAL	

Bills Payment *Calendar*

JAN ○ FEB ○ MAR ○ APR ○ MAY ○ JUN ○ JUL ○ AUG ○ SEP ○ OCT ○ NOV ○ DEC ○

SUN	MON	TUE	WED	THU	FRI	SAT

Debt Repayment *Plan*

JAN	FEB	MAR	APR	MAY	JUN	JUL	AUG	SEP	OCT	NOV	DEC
○	○	○	○	○	○	○	○	○	○	○	○

Creditor:	Debt Type:
Starting Balance:	Credit Limit:
Repayment Frequency:	Interest Rate:
Goal Pay Off Date:	Min Repayment:

DATE	REPAYMENT	BALANCE	NOTES

Expense *Tracker*

JAN ○ FEB ○ MAR ○ APR ○ MAY ○ JUN ○ JUL ○ AUG ○ SEP ○ OCT ○ NOV ○ DEC ○

DATE	DESCRIPTION	AMOUNT	NOTES

TOTAL ______________________

Credit Card *Tracker*

JAN ○ FEB ○ MAR ○ APR ○ MAY ○ JUN ○ JUL ○ AUG ○ SEP ○ OCT ○ NOV ○ DEC ○

DATE	CREDIT CARD	CREDIT LIMIT	%RATE	AMOUNT DUE	AMOUNT PAID	BALANCE

Monthly Financial *Reflection*

JAN ○ FEB ○ MAR ○ APR ○ MAY ○ JUN ○ JUL ○ AUG ○ SEP ○ OCT ○ NOV ○ DEC ○

TOTAL INCOME	TOTAL EXPENSES	DIFFERENCE	BALANCE

Biggest Wins this Month

What am I grateful for?

What do I need to improve for next month?

What did I learn by tracking my finances this month?

Wish *List*

JAN ○ FEB ○ MAR ○ APR ○ MAY ○ JUN ○ JUL ○ AUG ○ SEP ○ OCT ○ NOV ○ DEC ○

WISH LIST	HOPE TO PAY	WHERE TO BUY	BOUGHT	SPENT	SAVED	NOTES
			☐			
			☐			
			☐			
			☐			
			☐			
			☐			
			☐			
			☐			
			☐			
			☐			
			☐			
			☐			
			☐			
			☐			
			☐			
			☐			
			☐			
			☐			
			☐			
			☐			
			☐			
			☐			
			☐			
			☐			

Emergency Fund *Tracker*

JAN ○ FEB ○ MAR ○ APR ○ MAY ○ JUN ○ JUL ○ AUG ○ SEP ○ OCT ○ NOV ○ DEC ○

AMOUNT NEEDED:	TARGET DATE:
MONTHLY SAVINGS TARGET:	ACCOUNT:

Progress Tracker

10%	20%	30%	40%	50%	60%	70%	80%	90%	100%

DATE	DEPOSIT	WITHDRAW	NOTES	BALANCE

Notes

Credit Networking and *Mentorship*

JAN ○ FEB ○ MAR ○ APR ○ MAY ○ JUN ○ JUL ○ AUG ○ SEP ○ OCT ○ NOV ○ DEC ○

Networking Goals

What specific goals do you have for networking this month?

1 ______________________________

2 ______________________________

3 ______________________________

Mentorship Goals

What do you want to achieve with the help of a mentor this month?

1 ______________________________

2 ______________________________

3 ______________________________

Identify Networking Opportunities

Events & Workshops

List credit-related events, workshops, or webinars to attend this month:

1 ______________________________

2 ______________________________

3 ______________________________

Online Communities

Identify online groups or forums where you can engage with others focused on credit improvement:

1 ____________________

2 ____________________

3 ____________________

Track Your Progress

Networking Activities

Record your networking activities for the month (e.g., events attended, new connections made):

1 ____________________

2 ____________________

3 ____________________

Mentorship Activities:

Record your interactions with mentors (e.g., meetings, advice received):

1 ____________________

2 ____________________

3 ____________________

Notes

Charity and *Giving*

JAN ○ FEB ○ MAR ○ APR ○ MAY ○ JUN ○ JUL ○ AUG ○ SEP ○ OCT ○ NOV ○ DEC ○

DONATION	ORGANIZATION	DATE GIVEN	VALUE	TAX DEDUCTIBLE

Self-care and Financial *Health*

JAN ○ FEB ○ MAR ○ APR ○ MAY ○ JUN ○ JUL ○ AUG ○ SEP ○ OCT ○ NOV ○ DEC ○

Self-Care Reflection

- **Physical Well-being**

  What physical health activities will you focus on this month?

  o ______________________________

  o ______________________________

- **Emotional & Mental Wellness**

  What mental health activities will you focus on this month?

  o ______________________________

  o ______________________________

- **Time for Self-Care**

  How will you make time for yourself?

  o ______________________________

  o ______________________________

Financial Health Reflection

- **Current Financial Practices**

  What financial habits do you want to maintain or improve this month?

  o ______________________________

  o ______________________________

- **Financial Goals**

  List your financial goals for this month

  - o ______________________
  - o ______________________

- **Financial Self-Care**

  How will you manage financial stress?

  - o ______________________
  - o ______________________

Accountability & Progress

- **Support System**

  Who will help you stay accountable this month?

  - o ______________________
  - o ______________________

- **Tracking Progress**

  How will you monitor your progress? (e.g., weekly check-ins, journaling)

  - o ______________________
  - o ______________________

- **End-of-Month Review Date**

  Set a date to review your goals and make any necessary adjustments

  - o ______________________

August

SMART Financial Goals *Worksheet*

JAN ○ FEB ○ MAR ○ APR ○ MAY ○ JUN ○ JUL ○ AUG ○ SEP ○ OCT ○ NOV ○ DEC ○

Description of Goals					
SPECIFIC Cost					
MEASURABLE Monthly Amount					
ATTAINABLE Method/Steps					
REALISTIC Goal Length					
TIMEBOUND Your Timeline					

Notes

Monthly Budget *Planner*

JAN ○ FEB ○ MAR ○ APR ○ MAY ○ JUN ○ JUL ○ AUG ○ SEP ○ OCT ○ NOV ○ DEC ○

INCOME	AMOUNT
TOTAL	

BILLS	AMOUNT
TOTAL	

SAVINGS	AMOUNT
TOTAL	

EXPENSES	AMOUNT
TOTAL	

DEBT	AMOUNT
TOTAL	

SUMMARY	AMOUNT
INCOME	
BILLS	
SAVINGS	
EXPENSES	
DEBT	
TOTAL	

Bills Payment *Calendar*

JAN ○ FEB ○ MAR ○ APR ○ MAY ○ JUN ○ JUL ○ AUG ○ SEP ○ OCT ○ NOV ○ DEC ○

SUN	MON	TUE	WED	THU	FRI	SAT
○ ○	○ ○	○ ○	○ ○	○ ○	○ ○	○ ○
○ ○	○ ○	○ ○	○ ○	○ ○	○ ○	○ ○
○ ○	○ ○	○ ○	○ ○	○ ○	○ ○	○ ○
○ ○	○ ○	○ ○	○ ○	○ ○	○ ○	○ ○
○ ○	○ ○	○ ○	○ ○	○ ○	○ ○	○ ○

Debt Repayment *Plan*

JAN ○ FEB ○ MAR ○ APR ○ MAY ○ JUN ○ JUL ○ AUG ○ SEP ○ OCT ○ NOV ○ DEC ○

Creditor:	Debt Type:
Starting Balance:	Credit Limit:
Repayment Frequency:	Interest Rate:
Goal Pay Off Date:	Min Repayment:

DATE	REPAYMENT	BALANCE	NOTES

Expense *Tracker*

JAN ○ FEB ○ MAR ○ APR ○ MAY ○ JUN ○ JUL ○ AUG ○ SEP ○ OCT ○ NOV ○ DEC ○

DATE	DESCRIPTION	AMOUNT	NOTES

TOTAL ______________________

Credit Card *Tracker*

JAN ○ FEB ○ MAR ○ APR ○ MAY ○ JUN ○ JUL ○ AUG ○ SEP ○ OCT ○ NOV ○ DEC ○

DATE	CREDIT CARD	CREDIT LIMIT	%RATE	AMOUNT DUE	AMOUNT PAID	BALANCE

Monthly Financial *Reflection*

JAN ○ FEB ○ MAR ○ APR ○ MAY ○ JUN ○ JUL ○ AUG ○ SEP ○ OCT ○ NOV ○ DEC ○

TOTAL INCOME	TOTAL EXPENSES	DIFFERENCE	BALANCE

Biggest Wins this Month

What am I grateful for?

What do I need to improve for next month?

What did I learn by tracking my finances this month?

Wish *List*

JAN ○ FEB ○ MAR ○ APR ○ MAY ○ JUN ○ JUL ○ AUG ○ SEP ○ OCT ○ NOV ○ DEC ○

WISH LIST	HOPE TO PAY	WHERE TO BUY	BOUGHT	SPENT	SAVED	NOTES
			☐			
			☐			
			☐			
			☐			
			☐			
			☐			
			☐			
			☐			
			☐			
			☐			
			☐			
			☐			
			☐			
			☐			
			☐			
			☐			
			☐			
			☐			
			☐			
			☐			
			☐			
			☐			
			☐			
			☐			

Emergency Fund *Tracker*

JAN ○ FEB ○ MAR ○ APR ○ MAY ○ JUN ○ JUL ○ AUG ○ SEP ○ OCT ○ NOV ○ DEC ○

AMOUNT NEEDED:	TARGET DATE:
MONTHLY SAVINGS TARGET:	ACCOUNT:

Progress Tracker

10%	20%	30%	40%	50%	60%	70%	80%	90%	100%

DATE	DEPOSIT	WITHDRAW	NOTES	BALANCE

Notes

Credit Networking and *Mentorship*

JAN ○ FEB ○ MAR ○ APR ○ MAY ○ JUN ○ JUL ○ AUG ○ SEP ○ OCT ○ NOV ○ DEC ○

Networking Goals

What specific goals do you have for networking this month?

1 ______________________

2 ______________________

3 ______________________

Mentorship Goals

What do you want to achieve with the help of a mentor this month?

1 ______________________

2 ______________________

3 ______________________

Identify Networking Opportunities

Events & Workshops

List credit-related events, workshops, or webinars to attend this month:

1 ______________________

2 ______________________

3 ______________________

Online Communities

Identify online groups or forums where you can engage with others focused on credit improvement:

1 ______________________________

2 ______________________________

3 ______________________________

Track Your Progress

Networking Activities

Record your networking activities for the month (e.g., events attended, new connections made):

1 ______________________________

2 ______________________________

3 ______________________________

Mentorship Activities:

Record your interactions with mentors (e.g., meetings, advice received):

1 ______________________________

2 ______________________________

3 ______________________________

Notes

____

____

____

Charity and *Giving*

JAN ○ FEB ○ MAR ○ APR ○ MAY ○ JUN ○ JUL ○ AUG ○ SEP ○ OCT ○ NOV ○ DEC ○

DONATION	ORGANIZATION	DATE GIVEN	VALUE	TAX DEDUCTIBLE

Self-care and Financial *Health*

JAN ○ FEB ○ MAR ○ APR ○ MAY ○ JUN ○ JUL ○ AUG ○ SEP ○ OCT ○ NOV ○ DEC ○

Self-Care Reflection

- **Physical Well-being**

  What physical health activities will you focus on this month?

  o ______________________________

  o ______________________________

- **Emotional & Mental Wellness**

  What mental health activities will you focus on this month?

  o ______________________________

  o ______________________________

- **Time for Self-Care**

  How will you make time for yourself?

  o ______________________________

  o ______________________________

Financial Health Reflection

- **Current Financial Practices**

  What financial habits do you want to maintain or improve this month?

  o ______________________________

  o ______________________________

- **Financial Goals**

  List your financial goals for this month

  - o ______________________
  - o ______________________

- **Financial Self-Care**

  How will you manage financial stress?

  - o ______________________
  - o ______________________

Accountability & Progress

- **Support System**

  Who will help you stay accountable this month?

  - o ______________________
  - o ______________________

- **Tracking Progress**

  How will you monitor your progress? (e.g., weekly check-ins, journaling)

  - o ______________________
  - o ______________________

- **End-of-Month Review Date**

  Set a date to review your goals and make any necessary adjustments

  - o ______________________

September

SMART Financial Goals *Worksheet*

JAN ○ FEB ○ MAR ○ APR ○ MAY ○ JUN ○ JUL ○ AUG ○ SEP ○ OCT ○ NOV ○ DEC ○

Description of Goals					
SPECIFIC Cost					
MEASURABLE Monthly Amount					
ATTAINABLE Method/Steps					
REALISTIC Goal Length					
TIMEBOUND Your Timeline					

Notes

Monthly Budget *Planner*

JAN ○ FEB ○ MAR ○ APR ○ MAY ○ JUN ○ JUL ○ AUG ○ SEP ○ OCT ○ NOV ○ DEC ○

INCOME	AMOUNT
TOTAL	

BILLS	AMOUNT
TOTAL	

SAVINGS	AMOUNT
TOTAL	

EXPENSES	AMOUNT
TOTAL	

DEBT	AMOUNT
TOTAL	

SUMMARY	AMOUNT
INCOME	
BILLS	
SAVINGS	
EXPENSES	
DEBT	
TOTAL	

Bills Payment *Calendar*

JAN ○ FEB ○ MAR ○ APR ○ MAY ○ JUN ○ JUL ○ AUG ○ SEP ○ OCT ○ NOV ○ DEC ○

SUN	MON	TUE	WED	THU	FRI	SAT
○ ○	○ ○	○ ○	○ ○	○ ○	○ ○	○ ○
○ ○	○ ○	○ ○	○ ○	○ ○	○ ○	○ ○
○ ○	○ ○	○ ○	○ ○	○ ○	○ ○	○ ○
○ ○	○ ○	○ ○	○ ○	○ ○	○ ○	○ ○
○ ○	○ ○	○ ○	○ ○	○ ○	○ ○	○ ○

Debt Repayment *Plan*

JAN ○ FEB ○ MAR ○ APR ○ MAY ○ JUN ○ JUL ○ AUG ○ SEP ○ OCT ○ NOV ○ DEC ○

Creditor:	Debt Type:
Starting Balance:	Credit Limit:
Repayment Frequency:	Interest Rate:
Goal Pay Off Date:	Min Repayment:

DATE	REPAYMENT	BALANCE	NOTES

Expense *Tracker*

JAN ○ FEB ○ MAR ○ APR ○ MAY ○ JUN ○ JUL ○ AUG ○ SEP ○ OCT ○ NOV ○ DEC ○

DATE	DESCRIPTION	AMOUNT	NOTES

TOTAL ______________________

Credit Card *Tracker*

JAN ○ FEB ○ MAR ○ APR ○ MAY ○ JUN ○ JUL ○ AUG ○ SEP ○ OCT ○ NOV ○ DEC ○

DATE	CREDIT CARD	CREDIT LIMIT	%RATE	AMOUNT DUE	AMOUNT PAID	BALANCE

Monthly Financial *Reflection*

JAN ○ FEB ○ MAR ○ APR ○ MAY ○ JUN ○ JUL ○ AUG ○ SEP ○ OCT ○ NOV ○ DEC ○

TOTAL INCOME	TOTAL EXPENSES	DIFFERENCE	BALANCE

Biggest Wins this Month

What am I grateful for?

What do I need to improve for next month?

What did I learn by tracking my finances this month?

Wish *List*

JAN ○ FEB ○ MAR ○ APR ○ MAY ○ JUN ○ JUL ○ AUG ○ SEP ○ OCT ○ NOV ○ DEC ○

WISH LIST	HOPE TO PAY	WHERE TO BUY	BOUGHT	SPENT	SAVED	NOTES
			☐			
			☐			
			☐			
			☐			
			☐			
			☐			
			☐			
			☐			
			☐			
			☐			
			☐			
			☐			
			☐			
			☐			
			☐			
			☐			
			☐			
			☐			
			☐			
			☐			
			☐			
			☐			
			☐			
			☐			

Emergency Fund *Tracker*

JAN ○ FEB ○ MAR ○ APR ○ MAY ○ JUN ○ JUL ○ AUG ○ SEP ○ OCT ○ NOV ○ DEC ○

AMOUNT NEEDED:	TARGET DATE:
MONTHLY SAVINGS TARGET:	ACCOUNT:

Progress Tracker

10%	20%	30%	40%	50%	60%	70%	80%	90%	100%

DATE	DEPOSIT	WITHDRAW	NOTES	BALANCE

Notes

Credit Networking and *Mentorship*

JAN ○ FEB ○ MAR ○ APR ○ MAY ○ JUN ○ JUL ○ AUG ○ SEP ○ OCT ○ NOV ○ DEC ○

Networking Goals

What specific goals do you have for networking this month?

1 ______________________________

2 ______________________________

3 ______________________________

Mentorship Goals

What do you want to achieve with the help of a mentor this month?

1 ______________________________

2 ______________________________

3 ______________________________

Identify Networking Opportunities

Events & Workshops

List credit-related events, workshops, or webinars to attend this month:

1 ______________________________

2 ______________________________

3 ______________________________

Online Communities

Identify online groups or forums where you can engage with others focused on credit improvement:

1 ________________________________

2 ________________________________

3 ________________________________

Track Your Progress

Networking Activities

Record your networking activities for the month (e.g., events attended, new connections made):

1 ________________________________

2 ________________________________

3 ________________________________

Mentorship Activities:

Record your interactions with mentors (e.g., meetings, advice received):

1 ________________________________

2 ________________________________

3 ________________________________

Notes

Charity and *Giving*

JAN ○ FEB ○ MAR ○ APR ○ MAY ○ JUN ○ JUL ○ AUG ○ SEP ○ OCT ○ NOV ○ DEC ○

DONATION	ORGANIZATION	DATE GIVEN	VALUE	TAX DEDUCTIBLE

Self-care and Financial *Health*

JAN ○ FEB ○ MAR ○ APR ○ MAY ○ JUN ○ JUL ○ AUG ○ SEP ○ OCT ○ NOV ○ DEC ○

Self-Care Reflection

- **Physical Well-being**

  What physical health activities will you focus on this month?

  o ____

  o ____

- **Emotional & Mental Wellness**

  What mental health activities will you focus on this month?

  o ____

  o ____

- **Time for Self-Care**

  How will you make time for yourself?

  o ____

  o ____

Financial Health Reflection

- **Current Financial Practices**

  What financial habits do you want to maintain or improve this month?

  o ____

  o ____

- **Financial Goals**

  List your financial goals for this month

  o ______________________________

  o ______________________________

- **Financial Self-Care**

  How will you manage financial stress?

  o ______________________________

  o ______________________________

Accountability & Progress

- **Support System**

  Who will help you stay accountable this month?

  o ______________________________

  o ______________________________

- **Tracking Progress**

  How will you monitor your progress? (e.g., weekly check-ins, journaling)

  o ______________________________

  o ______________________________

- **End-of-Month Review Date**

  Set a date to review your goals and make any necessary adjustments

  o ______________________________

October

SMART Financial Goals *Worksheet*

JAN ○ FEB ○ MAR ○ APR ○ MAY ○ JUN ○ JUL ○ AUG ○ SEP ○ OCT ○ NOV ○ DEC ○

Description of Goals					
SPECIFIC Cost					
MEASURABLE Monthly Amount					
ATTAINABLE Method/Steps					
REALISTIC Goal Length					
TIMEBOUND Your Timeline					

Notes

Monthly Budget *Planner*

JAN ○ FEB ○ MAR ○ APR ○ MAY ○ JUN ○ JUL ○ AUG ○ SEP ○ OCT ○ NOV ○ DEC ○

INCOME	AMOUNT
TOTAL	

BILLS	AMOUNT
TOTAL	

SAVINGS	AMOUNT
TOTAL	

EXPENSES	AMOUNT
TOTAL	

DEBT	AMOUNT
TOTAL	

SUMMARY	AMOUNT
INCOME	
BILLS	
SAVINGS	
EXPENSES	
DEBT	
TOTAL	

Bills Payment *Calendar*

JAN ○ FEB ○ MAR ○ APR ○ MAY ○ JUN ○ JUL ○ AUG ○ SEP ○ OCT ○ NOV ○ DEC ○

SUN	MON	TUE	WED	THU	FRI	SAT

Debt Repayment *Plan*

JAN ○ FEB ○ MAR ○ APR ○ MAY ○ JUN ○ JUL ○ AUG ○ SEP ○ OCT ○ NOV ○ DEC ○

Creditor:	Debt Type:
Starting Balance:	Credit Limit:
Repayment Frequency:	Interest Rate:
Goal Pay Off Date:	Min Repayment:

DATE	REPAYMENT	BALANCE	NOTES

Expense *Tracker*

JAN ○ FEB ○ MAR ○ APR ○ MAY ○ JUN ○ JUL ○ AUG ○ SEP ○ OCT ○ NOV ○ DEC ○

DATE	DESCRIPTION	AMOUNT	NOTES

TOTAL ______________________

Credit Card *Tracker*

JAN ○ FEB ○ MAR ○ APR ○ MAY ○ JUN ○ JUL ○ AUG ○ SEP ○ OCT ○ NOV ○ DEC ○

DATE	CREDIT CARD	CREDIT LIMIT	%RATE	AMOUNT DUE	AMOUNT PAID	BALANCE

Monthly Financial *Reflection*

JAN ○ FEB ○ MAR ○ APR ○ MAY ○ JUN ○ JUL ○ AUG ○ SEP ○ OCT ○ NOV ○ DEC ○

TOTAL INCOME	TOTAL EXPENSES	DIFFERENCE	BALANCE

Biggest Wins this Month

What am I grateful for?

What do I need to improve for next month?

What did I learn by tracking my finances this month?

Wish *List*

JAN ○ FEB ○ MAR ○ APR ○ MAY ○ JUN ○ JUL ○ AUG ○ SEP ○ OCT ○ NOV ○ DEC ○

WISH LIST	HOPE TO PAY	WHERE TO BUY	BOUGHT	SPENT	SAVED	NOTES
			☐			
			☐			
			☐			
			☐			
			☐			
			☐			
			☐			
			☐			
			☐			
			☐			
			☐			
			☐			
			☐			
			☐			
			☐			
			☐			
			☐			
			☐			
			☐			
			☐			
			☐			
			☐			
			☐			
			☐			

Emergency Fund *Tracker*

JAN ○ FEB ○ MAR ○ APR ○ MAY ○ JUN ○ JUL ○ AUG ○ SEP ○ OCT ○ NOV ○ DEC ○

AMOUNT NEEDED:	TARGET DATE:
MONTHLY SAVINGS TARGET:	ACCOUNT:

Progress Tracker

10%	20%	30%	40%	50%	60%	70%	80%	90%	100%

DATE	DEPOSIT	WITHDRAW	NOTES	BALANCE

Notes

Credit Networking and *Mentorship*

JAN ○ FEB ○ MAR ○ APR ○ MAY ○ JUN ○ JUL ○ AUG ○ SEP ○ OCT ○ NOV ○ DEC ○

Networking Goals

What specific goals do you have for networking this month?

1 ______________________________

2 ______________________________

3 ______________________________

Mentorship Goals

What do you want to achieve with the help of a mentor this month?

1 ______________________________

2 ______________________________

3 ______________________________

Identify Networking Opportunities

Events & Workshops

List credit-related events, workshops, or webinars to attend this month:

1 ______________________________

2 ______________________________

3 ______________________________

Online Communities

Identify online groups or forums where you can engage with others focused on credit improvement:

1 ______________________________

2 ______________________________

3 ______________________________

Track Your Progress

Networking Activities

Record your networking activities for the month (e.g., events attended, new connections made):

1 ______________________________

2 ______________________________

3 ______________________________

Mentorship Activities:

Record your interactions with mentors (e.g., meetings, advice received):

1 ______________________________

2 ______________________________

3 ______________________________

Notes

____

____

____

Charity and *Giving*

JAN ○ FEB ○ MAR ○ APR ○ MAY ○ JUN ○ JUL ○ AUG ○ SEP ○ OCT ○ NOV ○ DEC ○

DONATION	ORGANIZATION	DATE GIVEN	VALUE	TAX DEDUCTIBLE

Self-care and Financial *Health*

JAN ○ FEB ○ MAR ○ APR ○ MAY ○ JUN ○ JUL ○ AUG ○ SEP ○ OCT ○ NOV ○ DEC ○

Self-Care Reflection

- **Physical Well-being**

  What physical health activities will you focus on this month?

  o ____

  o ____

- **Emotional & Mental Wellness**

  What mental health activities will you focus on this month?

  o ____

  o ____

- **Time for Self-Care**

  How will you make time for yourself?

  o ____

  o ____

Financial Health Reflection

- **Current Financial Practices**

  What financial habits do you want to maintain or improve this month?

  o ____

  o ____

- **Financial Goals**

  List your financial goals for this month

  - o ____
  - o ____

- **Financial Self-Care**

  How will you manage financial stress?

  - o ____
  - o ____

Accountability & Progress

- **Support System**

  Who will help you stay accountable this month?

  - o ____
  - o ____

- **Tracking Progress**

  How will you monitor your progress? (e.g., weekly check-ins, journaling)

  - o ____
  - o ____

- **End-of-Month Review Date**

  Set a date to review your goals and make any necessary adjustments

  - o ____

November

SMART Financial Goals *Worksheet*

JAN ○ FEB ○ MAR ○ APR ○ MAY ○ JUN ○ JUL ○ AUG ○ SEP ○ OCT ○ NOV ○ DEC ○

Description of Goals					
SPECIFIC Cost					
MEASURABLE Monthly Amount					
ATTAINABLE Method/Steps					
REALISTIC Goal Length					
TIMEBOUND Your Timeline					

Notes

Monthly Budget *Planner*

JAN ○ FEB ○ MAR ○ APR ○ MAY ○ JUN ○ JUL ○ AUG ○ SEP ○ OCT ○ NOV ○ DEC ○

INCOME	AMOUNT
TOTAL	

BILLS	AMOUNT
TOTAL	

SAVINGS	AMOUNT
TOTAL	

EXPENSES	AMOUNT
TOTAL	

DEBT	AMOUNT
TOTAL	

SUMMARY	AMOUNT
INCOME	
BILLS	
SAVINGS	
EXPENSES	
DEBT	
TOTAL	

Bills Payment *Calendar*

JAN ○ FEB ○ MAR ○ APR ○ MAY ○ JUN ○ JUL ○ AUG ○ SEP ○ OCT ○ NOV ○ DEC ○

SUN	MON	TUE	WED	THU	FRI	SAT
○ ○	○ ○	○ ○	○ ○	○ ○	○ ○	○ ○
○ ○	○ ○	○ ○	○ ○	○ ○	○ ○	○ ○
○ ○	○ ○	○ ○	○ ○	○ ○	○ ○	○ ○
○ ○	○ ○	○ ○	○ ○	○ ○	○ ○	○ ○
○ ○	○ ○	○ ○	○ ○	○ ○	○ ○	○ ○

Debt Repayment *Plan*

JAN ○ FEB ○ MAR ○ APR ○ MAY ○ JUN ○ JUL ○ AUG ○ SEP ○ OCT ○ NOV ○ DEC ○

Creditor:	Debt Type:
Starting Balance:	Credit Limit:
Repayment Frequency:	Interest Rate:
Goal Pay Off Date:	Min Repayment:

DATE	REPAYMENT	BALANCE	NOTES

Expense *Tracker*

JAN ○ FEB ○ MAR ○ APR ○ MAY ○ JUN ○ JUL ○ AUG ○ SEP ○ OCT ○ NOV ○ DEC ○

DATE	DESCRIPTION	AMOUNT	NOTES

TOTAL ______________________

Credit Card *Tracker*

JAN ○ FEB ○ MAR ○ APR ○ MAY ○ JUN ○ JUL ○ AUG ○ SEP ○ OCT ○ NOV ○ DEC ○

DATE	CREDIT CARD	CREDIT LIMIT	%RATE	AMOUNT DUE	AMOUNT PAID	BALANCE

Monthly Financial *Reflection*

JAN ○ FEB ○ MAR ○ APR ○ MAY ○ JUN ○ JUL ○ AUG ○ SEP ○ OCT ○ NOV ○ DEC ○

TOTAL INCOME	TOTAL EXPENSES	DIFFERENCE	BALANCE

Biggest Wins this Month

What am I grateful for?

What do I need to improve for next month?

What did I learn by tracking my finances this month?

Wish *List*

JAN ○ FEB ○ MAR ○ APR ○ MAY ○ JUN ○ JUL ○ AUG ○ SEP ○ OCT ○ NOV ○ DEC ○

WISH LIST	HOPE TO PAY	WHERE TO BUY	BOUGHT	SPENT	SAVED	NOTES
			☐			
			☐			
			☐			
			☐			
			☐			
			☐			
			☐			
			☐			
			☐			
			☐			
			☐			
			☐			
			☐			
			☐			
			☐			
			☐			
			☐			
			☐			
			☐			
			☐			
			☐			
			☐			
			☐			
			☐			

Emergency Fund *Tracker*

JAN ○ FEB ○ MAR ○ APR ○ MAY ○ JUN ○ JUL ○ AUG ○ SEP ○ OCT ○ NOV ○ DEC ○

AMOUNT NEEDED:	TARGET DATE:
MONTHLY SAVINGS TARGET:	ACCOUNT:

Progress Tracker

10%	20%	30%	40%	50%	60%	70%	80%	90%	100%

DATE	DEPOSIT	WITHDRAW	NOTES	BALANCE

Notes

Credit Networking and *Mentorship*

JAN ○ FEB ○ MAR ○ APR ○ MAY ○ JUN ○ JUL ○ AUG ○ SEP ○ OCT ○ NOV ○ DEC ○

Networking Goals

What specific goals do you have for networking this month?

1 ____________________

2 ____________________

3 ____________________

Mentorship Goals

What do you want to achieve with the help of a mentor this month?

1 ____________________

2 ____________________

3 ____________________

Identify Networking Opportunities

Events & Workshops

List credit-related events, workshops, or webinars to attend this month:

1 ____________________

2 ____________________

3 ____________________

Online Communities

Identify online groups or forums where you can engage with others focused on credit improvement:

1 ______________________________

2 ______________________________

3 ______________________________

Track Your Progress

Networking Activities

Record your networking activities for the month (e.g., events attended, new connections made):

1 ______________________________

2 ______________________________

3 ______________________________

Mentorship Activities:

Record your interactions with mentors (e.g., meetings, advice received):

1 ______________________________

2 ______________________________

3 ______________________________

Notes

____

____

____

Charity and *Giving*

JAN ○ FEB ○ MAR ○ APR ○ MAY ○ JUN ○ JUL ○ AUG ○ SEP ○ OCT ○ NOV ○ DEC ○

DONATION	ORGANIZATION	DATE GIVEN	VALUE	TAX DEDUCTIBLE

Self-care and Financial *Health*

JAN ○ FEB ○ MAR ○ APR ○ MAY ○ JUN ○ JUL ○ AUG ○ SEP ○ OCT ○ NOV ○ DEC ○

Self-Care Reflection

- **Physical Well-being**

  What physical health activities will you focus on this month?

  o ______________________________

  o ______________________________

- **Emotional & Mental Wellness**

  What mental health activities will you focus on this month?

  o ______________________________

  o ______________________________

- **Time for Self-Care**

  How will you make time for yourself?

  o ______________________________

  o ______________________________

Financial Health Reflection

- **Current Financial Practices**

  What financial habits do you want to maintain or improve this month?

  o ______________________________

  o ______________________________

- **Financial Goals**

  List your financial goals for this month

  - o ______
  - o ______

- **Financial Self-Care**

  How will you manage financial stress?

  - o ______
  - o ______

Accountability & Progress

- **Support System**

  Who will help you stay accountable this month?

  - o ______
  - o ______

- **Tracking Progress**

  How will you monitor your progress? (e.g., weekly check-ins, journaling)

  - o ______
  - o ______

- **End-of-Month Review Date**

  Set a date to review your goals and make any necessary adjustments

  - o ______

December

SMART Financial Goals *Worksheet*

JAN ○ FEB ○ MAR ○ APR ○ MAY ○ JUN ○ JUL ○ AUG ○ SEP ○ OCT ○ NOV ○ DEC ○

Description of Goals					
SPECIFIC Cost					
MEASURABLE Monthly Amount					
ATTAINABLE Method/Steps					
REALISTIC Goal Length					
TIMEBOUND Your Timeline					

Notes

Monthly Budget *Planner*

JAN ○ FEB ○ MAR ○ APR ○ MAY ○ JUN ○ JUL ○ AUG ○ SEP ○ OCT ○ NOV ○ DEC ○

INCOME	AMOUNT
TOTAL	

BILLS	AMOUNT
TOTAL	

SAVINGS	AMOUNT
TOTAL	

EXPENSES	AMOUNT
TOTAL	

DEBT	AMOUNT
TOTAL	

SUMMARY	AMOUNT
INCOME	
BILLS	
SAVINGS	
EXPENSES	
DEBT	
TOTAL	

Bills Payment *Calendar*

JAN ○ FEB ○ MAR ○ APR ○ MAY ○ JUN ○ JUL ○ AUG ○ SEP ○ OCT ○ NOV ○ DEC ○

SUN	MON	TUE	WED	THU	FRI	SAT
○ ○	○ ○	○ ○	○ ○	○ ○	○ ○	○ ○
○ ○	○ ○	○ ○	○ ○	○ ○	○ ○	○ ○
○ ○	○ ○	○ ○	○ ○	○ ○	○ ○	○ ○
○ ○	○ ○	○ ○	○ ○	○ ○	○ ○	○ ○
○ ○	○ ○	○ ○	○ ○	○ ○	○ ○	○ ○

Debt Repayment *Plan*

JAN ○ FEB ○ MAR ○ APR ○ MAY ○ JUN ○ JUL ○ AUG ○ SEP ○ OCT ○ NOV ○ DEC ○

Creditor:	Debt Type:
Starting Balance:	Credit Limit:
Repayment Frequency:	Interest Rate:
Goal Pay Off Date:	Min Repayment:

DATE	REPAYMENT	BALANCE	NOTES

Expense *Tracker*

JAN ○ FEB ○ MAR ○ APR ○ MAY ○ JUN ○ JUL ○ AUG ○ SEP ○ OCT ○ NOV ○ DEC ○

DATE	DESCRIPTION	AMOUNT	NOTES

TOTAL ____________________

Credit Card *Tracker*

JAN ○ FEB ○ MAR ○ APR ○ MAY ○ JUN ○ JUL ○ AUG ○ SEP ○ OCT ○ NOV ○ DEC ○

DATE	CREDIT CARD	CREDIT LIMIT	%RATE	AMOUNT DUE	AMOUNT PAID	BALANCE

Monthly Financial *Reflection*

JAN ○ FEB ○ MAR ○ APR ○ MAY ○ JUN ○ JUL ○ AUG ○ SEP ○ OCT ○ NOV ○ DEC ○

TOTAL INCOME	TOTAL EXPENSES	DIFFERENCE	BALANCE

Biggest Wins this Month

What am I grateful for?

What do I need to improve for next month?

What did I learn by tracking my finances this month?

Wish *List*

JAN ○ FEB ○ MAR ○ APR ○ MAY ○ JUN ○ JUL ○ AUG ○ SEP ○ OCT ○ NOV ○ DEC ○

WISH LIST	HOPE TO PAY	WHERE TO BUY	BOUGHT	SPENT	SAVED	NOTES
			☐			
			☐			
			☐			
			☐			
			☐			
			☐			
			☐			
			☐			
			☐			
			☐			
			☐			
			☐			
			☐			
			☐			
			☐			
			☐			
			☐			
			☐			
			☐			
			☐			
			☐			
			☐			
			☐			
			☐			

Emergency Fund *Tracker*

JAN ○ FEB ○ MAR ○ APR ○ MAY ○ JUN ○ JUL ○ AUG ○ SEP ○ OCT ○ NOV ○ DEC ○

AMOUNT NEEDED:	TARGET DATE:
MONTHLY SAVINGS TARGET:	ACCOUNT:

Progress Tracker

10%	20%	30%	40%	50%	60%	70%	80%	90%	100%

DATE	DEPOSIT	WITHDRAW	NOTES	BALANCE

Notes

Credit Networking and *Mentorship*

JAN ○ FEB ○ MAR ○ APR ○ MAY ○ JUN ○ JUL ○ AUG ○ SEP ○ OCT ○ NOV ○ DEC ○

Networking Goals

What specific goals do you have for networking this month?

1 ____________________________________

2 ____________________________________

3 ____________________________________

Mentorship Goals

What do you want to achieve with the help of a mentor this month?

1 ____________________________________

2 ____________________________________

3 ____________________________________

Identify Networking Opportunities

Events & Workshops

List credit-related events, workshops, or webinars to attend this month:

1 ____________________________________

2 ____________________________________

3 ____________________________________

Online Communities

Identify online groups or forums where you can engage with others focused on credit improvement:

1 ______________________________

2 ______________________________

3 ______________________________

Track Your Progress

Networking Activities

Record your networking activities for the month (e.g., events attended, new connections made):

1 ______________________________

2 ______________________________

3 ______________________________

Mentorship Activities:

Record your interactions with mentors (e.g., meetings, advice received):

1 ______________________________

2 ______________________________

3 ______________________________

Notes

____

____

____

Charity and *Giving*

JAN ○ FEB ○ MAR ○ APR ○ MAY ○ JUN ○ JUL ○ AUG ○ SEP ○ OCT ○ NOV ○ DEC ○

DONATION	ORGANIZATION	DATE GIVEN	VALUE	TAX DEDUCTIBLE

Self-care and Financial *Health*

JAN ○ FEB ○ MAR ○ APR ○ MAY ○ JUN ○ JUL ○ AUG ○ SEP ○ OCT ○ NOV ○ DEC ○

Self-Care Reflection

- **Physical Well-being**

  What physical health activities will you focus on this month?

  - ______________________________
  - ______________________________

- **Emotional & Mental Wellness**

  What mental health activities will you focus on this month?

  - ______________________________
  - ______________________________

- **Time for Self-Care**

  How will you make time for yourself?

  - ______________________________
  - ______________________________

Financial Health Reflection

- **Current Financial Practices**

  What financial habits do you want to maintain or improve this month?

  - ______________________________
  - ______________________________

- **Financial Goals**

  List your financial goals for this month

  - o ____________________
  - o ____________________

- **Financial Self-Care**

  How will you manage financial stress?

  - o ____________________
  - o ____________________

Accountability & Progress

- **Support System**

  Who will help you stay accountable this month?

  - o ____________________
  - o ____________________

- **Tracking Progress**

  How will you monitor your progress? (e.g., weekly check-ins, journaling)

  - o ____________________
  - o ____________________

- **End-of-Month Review Date**

  Set a date to review your goals and make any necessary adjustments

  - o ____________________

Glossary of *Terms*

APR (Annual Percentage Rate): The annual interest rate charged on borrowed money, expressed as a percentage. For credit cards and loans, the APR represents the yearly cost of borrowing if you carry a balance or take out a loan.

Balance: The total amount of money owed on a credit card or loan at any given time. This includes any purchases made, interest charged, and fees applied.

Credit: The ability to borrow money or access goods and services with the understanding that you'll repay the lender later, often with interest.

Credit Bureau: A company that collects and maintains credit information for individuals. The three main credit bureaus in the U.S. are Experian, Equifax, and TransUnion. They issue credit reports that lenders use to assess creditworthiness.

Credit Card: A plastic or digital card that allows you to borrow funds from a bank or financial institution to make purchases. Credit cards come with a set limit and require repayment with potential interest if the balance isn't paid in full.

Credit History: A record of your borrowing and repayment behavior, including any loans, credit card accounts, and payments made. A positive credit history can help you get better loan terms in the future.

Credit Limit: The maximum amount of money you can borrow using a credit card. Staying below this limit and paying off balances promptly helps maintain good credit.

Credit Monitoring: A service that tracks your credit report and alerts you to any changes, such as new accounts opened in your name or significant shifts in your credit score. It helps protect against identity theft and fraud.

Credit Report: A detailed statement provided by a credit bureau that includes your credit history, including loan balances, payment history, credit inquiries, and public records such as bankruptcies. Lenders use this to assess your creditworthiness.

Credit Score: A three-digit number that summarizes your creditworthiness. It's based on your credit history and is used by lenders to assess your risk as a borrower. The higher the score, the better your credit.

Default: Failure to make the required payments on a loan or credit account for an extended period, often leading to penalties, a damaged credit score, and legal action from lenders.

Delinquency: A missed payment on a loan or credit card. If you're delinquent for too long, it can damage your credit score and lead to late fees or even default.

Dispute Process: The process of challenging inaccuracies or errors on your credit report. If a mistake is found, you can dispute it with the credit bureau, and they are required to investigate and correct the information if needed.

FICO Score: A type of credit score created by the Fair Isaac Corporation (FICO). It's one of the most widely used credit scores by lenders to determine credit risk. FICO scores range from 300 to 850.

Financial Aid: Money provided to students to help pay for college, which may include scholarships, grants, loans, and work-study programs. FAFSA is the main application for federal financial aid in the U.S.

Grace Period: The time after the due date of a credit card bill or loan payment during which no interest or late fees are charged. For federal student loans, the grace period typically lasts six months after you leave school.

Hard Inquiry (Hard Pull): A check into your credit history by a lender when you apply for credit. Multiple hard inquiries in a short period can temporarily lower your credit score.

Interest Rate: The percentage charged on borrowed money. It's the cost of borrowing and can vary depending on the type of loan, credit score, and other factors.

Loan: A sum of money borrowed from a lender with the expectation that it will be repaid with interest over a specified period. Common types include student loans, auto loans, and personal loans.

Minimum Payment: The smallest amount you must pay on your credit card or loan balance each month to keep your account in good standing. Paying only the minimum can lead to higher interest charges over time.

Principal: The original amount of money borrowed on a loan or invested, not including interest. When you repay a loan, part of your payment goes toward reducing the principal, and part goes toward interest.

Repayment Plan: An agreement between a borrower and lender that outlines how a loan will be paid back, including the amount of monthly payments and the time frame for repayment. Common repayment plans for student loans include standard, income-driven, and extended.

Secured Credit Card: A type of credit card that requires a cash deposit to act as collateral. It's often used to build or rebuild credit. The deposit usually serves as the credit limit.

Soft Inquiry (Soft Pull): A check on your credit report that doesn't affect your credit score. Soft pulls occur when you check your own credit, or when lenders preapprove you for credit offers.

Student Loan: A type of loan specifically designed to help students pay for education-related expenses, including tuition, books, and living costs. Student loans can be federal or private and typically have lower interest rates than other loans.

Subsidized Loan: A federal student loan for which the government pays the interest while you're in school, during the grace period, and during any periods of deferment. These loans are based on financial need.

Unsecured Loan: A loan that doesn't require collateral (such as a house or car) for approval. Credit cards and personal loans are common examples. Interest rates on unsecured loans may be higher since the lender is taking on more risk.

Variable Interest Rate: An interest rate on a loan or credit card that can fluctuate over time based on market conditions. Variable rates can rise or fall, affecting the cost of borrowing.

Work-Study: A federal financial aid program that allows students to earn money through part-time employment while in school. Work-study funds are typically used to help pay education-related expenses.

Annual Fee: A yearly charge by some credit card companies for the use of a credit card. Some cards have no annual fees, while others offer rewards and benefits in exchange for the fee.

Authorized User: A person who is added to a credit card account and can use the card but is not legally responsible for the payments. Being an authorized user on someone else's account can help build your credit score if the account is managed responsibly.

Bankruptcy: A legal process through which individuals or businesses who cannot repay debts seek relief from some or all of their liabilities. Bankruptcy can severely damage your credit and make it difficult to obtain new credit in the future.

Cash Advance: A service provided by most credit card companies that allows cardholders to withdraw cash, typically from an ATM. Cash advances often come with high fees and interest rates, and they start accruing interest immediately.

Charge-Off: When a creditor writes off a debt because it is considered unlikely to be collected. Charge-offs can significantly harm your credit score and stay on your credit report for up to seven years.

Co-Signer: A person who agrees to take responsibility for repaying a loan if the primary borrower cannot. Co-signers can help borrowers qualify for loans they might not otherwise get, but they are equally responsible for the debt.

Collection Account: A debt that has been transferred to a collection agency after the original creditor was unable to collect payment. Collection accounts can severely damage your credit score and stay on your credit report for up to seven years.

Credit Counseling: A service that provides advice and education on managing debt, creating a budget, and improving credit. Credit counseling agencies can help people develop debt repayment plans and may work with creditors to reduce interest rates or monthly payments.

Credit Freeze: A service offered by credit bureaus that prevents new lenders from accessing your credit report, typically to prevent identity theft. You can temporarily lift the freeze if you need to apply for credit.

Credit Utilization Ratio: The percentage of your total available credit that you're using. A lower credit utilization ratio (below 30%) is better for your credit score. For example, if you have a credit limit of $1,000 and a balance of $300, your credit utilization ratio is 30%.

Debt-to-Income Ratio (DTI): The percentage of your monthly income that goes toward paying debts. Lenders use this ratio to determine your ability to manage monthly payments and repay debts. A lower DTI ratio is better for obtaining loans.

Deferment: A temporary pause on loan payments, often available for student loans. During deferment, interest may not accrue on subsidized loans, but it may continue to accrue on unsubsidized loans.

Direct Deposit: An electronic transfer of funds directly into a bank account, typically from an employer or government agency. It's a fast and convenient way to receive payments like paychecks or financial aid disbursements.

Due Date: The date by which a loan or credit card payment must be made to avoid late fees and penalties. Missing due dates can hurt your credit score and lead to higher interest rates.

Emergency Fund: A savings account set aside for unexpected expenses, such as medical bills or car repairs. Financial experts recommend having 3 to 6 months' worth of living expenses saved in your emergency fund.

Fixed Interest Rate: An interest rate on a loan or credit card that remains constant over the life of the loan. Fixed rates offer stability, as you know what your payment will be each month.

Forbearance: A temporary postponement or reduction of loan payments, often used for student loans when borrowers are facing financial hardship. Interest typically continues to accrue during forbearance.

Hardship Program: A repayment plan offered by lenders to help borrowers facing financial difficulties. These programs may reduce monthly payments, lower interest rates, or offer other assistance to prevent default.

Income-Driven Repayment Plan: A repayment option for federal student loans where monthly payments are based on your income and family size. These plans aim to make payments more affordable, and after 20-25 years, any remaining loan balance may be forgiven.

Late Payment: A payment that is not made by the due date. Late payments can result in fees and interest rate increases, and they may be reported to credit bureaus, damaging your credit score.

Loan Consolidation: The process of combining multiple loans into a single loan with one monthly payment. For federal student loans, this is known as Direct Consolidation, which can simplify repayment and may extend the loan term.

Overdraft: When you spend more money than is available in your bank account, causing the account balance to go negative. Overdrafts can result in fees and may affect your relationship with the bank.

Over-the-Limit Fee: A fee charged when your balance exceeds the credit limit on your credit card. This fee can be avoided by monitoring your balance and staying below your credit limit.

Payment History: A record of your past payments on credit accounts, including whether they were made on time, late, or missed. Payment history is a significant factor in determining your credit score.

Penalty APR: A higher interest rate charged on a credit card if you violate the terms of the account, such as by making late payments or exceeding your credit limit. The penalty APR can significantly increase the cost of carrying a balance.

Revolving Credit: A type of credit, such as a credit card, that allows you to borrow up to a certain limit and pay it off over time. As you repay the balance, you can borrow again, up to the credit limit.

Secured Loan: A loan that is backed by collateral, such as a car or home, which the lender can claim if the borrower fails to repay the loan. Secured loans typically have lower interest rates because they pose less risk to lenders.

Statement Balance: The total amount owed on a credit card at the end of a billing cycle. Paying the statement balance in full by the due date allows you to avoid interest charges.

Zero-Percent APR: A promotional offer by some credit card companies that temporarily allows cardholders to make purchases or balance transfers without paying interest. These offers typically last 6 to 18 months, after which a regular APR applies.

Made in United States
Orlando, FL
05 November 2026

90229437R00146